AMERICAN EVANGELICALS FOR TRUMP

D1571560

This book introduces the American Evangelical movement and the role it played in the support of Donald Trump. Specifically, it focuses on some Neocharismatic-Pentecostal (NCP) leaders, their beliefs, and their political strategies. The author examines why 81% of white evangelicals voted for Trump in 2016, and why he still received between 76% and 81% of their vote in 2020 despite losing the presidency. Additionally, the book discusses how NCP leaders are part of the Christian Right, a religious coalition with a political agenda centered on controversial issues such as anti-abortion activism, opposition to LGBTQ+ rights, and the protection of their religious freedom.

Structured around the three main ideas inspiring NCP leaders who supported Trump in 2016 and 2020—Dominion, Spiritual Warfare, and Eschatology (the End Times)—the book examines how these ideas have sustained the evangelicals close to U.S. political power in the Trump era. In light of the potential for Trump's return to power in 2024, the book serves as a warning of what a renewed alliance between Trump and his former NCP supporters could bring.

It is an essential read for all students and researchers of Evangelicalism, Religion in America, Political Theology, or Religion and Politics.

André Gagné is a Full Professor in the Department of Theological Studies at Concordia University, Montreal, Canada.

Translated by Linda Shanahan, a retired adjunct professor of physics, engineering, and mathematics from Buffalo, New York, U.S.A.

AMERICAN EVANGELICALS FOR TRUMP

Dominion, Spiritual Warfare, and the End Times

André Gagné

Translated by Linda Shanahan

Routledge
Taylor & Francis Group

LONDON AND NEW YORK

Designed cover image: Bloomberg / Contributor

First published 2024
by Routledge
4 Park Square, Milton Park, Abingdon, Oxon OX14 4RN

and by Routledge
605 Third Avenue, New York, NY 10158

Routledge is an imprint of the Taylor & Francis Group, an informa business

American Evangelicals for Trump, by André Gagné, originally published as *Ces évangéliques derrière Trump,* 2020

Authorised English Translation © 2024 Taylor & Francis, from the French language edition published by Les Éditions Labor et Fides, 2020

British Library Cataloguing-in-Publication Data
A catalogue record for this book is available from the British Library

ISBN: 978-1-032-41569-7 (hbk)
ISBN: 978-1-032-41568-0 (pbk)
ISBN: 978-1-003-35871-8 (ebk)

DOI: 10.4324/9781003358718

Typeset in Sabon
by MPS Limited, Dehradun

CONTENTS

PREFACE

André Gagné

This publication is an English translation[1] of my 2020 book, *Ces évangéliques derrière Trump: Hégémonie, démonologie et fin du monde* (Enquêtes 6),[2] published in French by Labor et Fides.[3] In mid-February 2020, I was invited by Philippe Gonzalez and Yannick Fer[4] to write a book for their series on American evangelical Trump supporters. The manuscript was to be submitted by the end of May 2020 so the book could be published in early Fall, just prior to the 2020 election in November. I had been researching and collecting a copious amount of information about Trump's evangelical supporters since 2016. I had all the content necessary for the book; now, I just needed to present my findings in a scholarly but accessible way. *Enquêtes* was the perfect venue for such a project.

What This Book Is Not About

There have been numerous important books[5] published recently by journalists, activists, and scholars on the influence of media, money, and the Religious Right in American politics,[6] Christian nationalism,[7] Evangelicals and their views on masculinity[8] and complementarianism,[9] Evangelical history leading to Trump,[10] and White Evangelical racism.[11] My book, therefore, does not address topics discussed by more competent scholars than I on race and gender in American evangelicalism, nor does it cover conservative Christian right organizations such as the Council for National Policy (CNP). I also do not frame the politics of U.S. Christians in terms of Christian nationalism, something which many scholars have already done in their work.

What This Book Is About

This book focuses on a segment of Trump evangelical supporters which has not been thoroughly examined: Neocharismatic-Pentecostal (NCP)[12] leaders and their theology, as well as their philosophy of political power. My research is sociotheological[13] in nature, and I use digital ethnography[14] and discourse analysis[15] in the study of primary sources.[16] In researching NCPs, the main focus needs to be on the way adherents speak about their beliefs and practices, rather than on imposing one's own analytical categories to explain the phenomenon, as argued by Birgit Meyer in her research on Global Pentecostalism,

> Resisting a reductive approach to religion, this methodology grounds scholarly analysis on Pentecostals' own views and practices. Obviously, such an approach resonates well with anthropological modes of research and knowledge production and is conducive to multidisciplinary cooperation with scholars in religious studies and theology. It can safely be stated that the most insightful scholarship on Pentecostalism is based on a successful translation of 'internal' into 'external' perspectives, taking as a point of departure what people believe and experience. The strength of this approach is that, rather than impose a neutral analytical language, it stays close to Pentecostalism's own vocabulary and does not solely explain its success by referring to nonreligious factors.[17]

To my knowledge, no other book has provided an analysis of the theological underpinnings of Trump's NCP supporters.[18] As we are now fast approaching the 2024 elections, this book should serve as a reminder of the past and present support of NCPs for Trump, their involvement in American politics, and their desire for political power.

In this book, I not only analyze the beliefs and practices of some key NCP Trump supporters, but I also examine some of the events which took place between the time of Trump's 2016 election and the end of May 2020. Some of the events which transpired subsequent to the original French version of my book and the issues they raised will be briefly addressed in an epilogue including the results of the 2020 elections, the January 6th insurrection,[19] the failed prophecies concerning Trump's re-election, the rift among Charismatics regarding political prophecies,[20] the ReAwaken America Tour, the reversal of *Roe vs. Wade*, and the 2022 mid-term elections. I will also explain what happened to key NCP leaders after Trump's defeat in 2020, and what can be understood as Trump's political legacy.

The U.S. Context and the Longer History of Pentecostal-Charismatic Christianity

This book does not provide an exhaustive look at the place of NCPs in the longer history of Charismatic Christianity. In explaining the various "Waves of the Spirit," the main focus is on the American context and I do not address, for example, questions about the polygenesis of Pentecostalism[21] nor the reported manifestation of spiritual gifts at earlier times.[22] In terms of the longer history of Pentecostal-Charismatic Christianity and the current U.S. context, I would like to address a few issues concerning the New Apostolic Reformation (NAR), the role of Apostles, the political theology of Dominion, and Eschatology.

On the NAR and Apostles

As to the New Apostolic Reformation (NAR)[23] discussed in several chapters of this book, my attention is focused on some leaders of Charismatic influence in the United States. C. Peter Wagner coined and applied the term "New Apostolic Reformation" to describe "the process of change in the Church" which he "traced back to around 1900."[24] In the foreword of an important anthology on Apostleship,[25] Wagner explained more precisely how his research lead him "to believe that the New Apostolic Reformation began around 1900 and that here in North America the Second Apostolic Age began in 2001."[26] Wagner clearly understood the "first component *of the NAR*" to be the African Independent Church movement (around 1900). The "second component" was the Chinese rural house church movement (mid-1970s), and the "third large component *of the NAR*" was the grassroots church movement in Latin America (also in the 1970s).[27] For Wagner, all these movements were believed to be *part of the NAR*, outside the United States. He also maintained that "God attempted to introduce the apostolic movement into North America in the years following World War II"—likely an implicit reference to the emergence of the New Order of the Latter Rain (NOLR), in 1948. Afterward, for about 30 years, "the apostolic movement faded in North America," and would later only be sustained by the independent charismatic church movement (in the 1970s).[28] Wagner claimed that the U.S. church[29] had entered a new historical season in 2001 which he called "the Second Apostolic Age."[30] Consequently, *sensu stricto*, Wagner did *not* see himself as the founder of the NAR, but rather coined the term "New Apostolic Reformation" to describe something that he believed *already* existed: the impetus of a new mode of ecclesiology which focused on apostolic leadership and networks. What Wagner *did* create, however, were networks to sustain the NAR both in the U.S. context and globally.

Although my book focuses on some leaders of Charismatic influence, it is important to note that for Wagner, the NAR movement also included individuals and churches that "are not all charismatic in orientation."[31] This diversity is confirmed by Joseph Mattera, former convening Apostle of the United States Coalition of Apostolic Leaders (USCAL): "there are Non-Charismatics in this movement. It's a diverse movement whose members have various views on eschatology, ecclesiology, leadership style."[32] In fact, Wagner's first edited book dedicated to the study of the NAR was titled *The New Apostolic Churches* and was published in 1998. Wagner explained that this book was part of a new season of research "focusing on the New Apostolic Reformation." Wagner's two previous seasons of research were dedicated to church growth (1970–1980) and to signs and wonders (1980–1995). *The New Apostolic Churches* was the result of a major conference on the "post-denominational church" in May 1996, at the Lake Avenue Congregational Church in Pasadena. The foreword to Wagner's edited book was written by Elmer L. Towns, a non-charismatic and co-founder of Liberty University. Another non-charismatic, Bill Hybels, founder and former pastor of Willow Creek Community Church, also contributed a chapter to Wagner's book.[33] The place of non-charismatic leaders and churches[34] aligns with Wagner's understanding of apostolic leadership and networks. In 1999, Wagner estimated that in the United States, 80% of new apostolic churches were charismatic, while 20% were non-charismatic. Examples given by Wagner of non-charismatic churches at the time were the Crystal Cathedral (Garden Grove, California), Willow Creek Community Church (South Barrington, Illinois), Saddleback Valley Community Church (Lake Forest, California), Community Church of Joy (Glendale, Arizona), and Frazer Memorial United Methodist Church (Montgomery, Alabama).[35]

The NAR, according to Wagner, is the most radical change in how churches operate since the Protestant Reformation. Its main characteristic relates to the "amount of spiritual authority delegated by the Holy Spirit to individuals."[36] This quality is also, therefore, applicable to non-charismatic church leaders. For example, Wagner labeled Bill Hybels as a "new apostolic pastor"[37] and said that Rick Warren was the pastor of a "new apostolic church."[38]

Wagner also tended to attribute apostolic leadership to Charismatic leaders who did not necessarily share his outlook. For example, he dedicated his first book on the NAR, *The New Apostolic Churches* (1998), to John Wimber, whom he believed had "apostolic authority" and was "a pioneer of the New Apostolic Reformation,"[39] despite the fact that Wimber "wanted to stay away from anything that hinted at restorationism (the notion that God is restoring the fivefold offices … the last being the office of the apostle)."[40]

On Dominion and Eschatology

On the issues of dominion and eschatology, I present these ideas in the context of the United States. Regarding dominion theology, Wagner specifically mentioned the influence of Rushdoony.[41] But the goal of social transformation was not always referred to in terms of dominion, as American Christians had been seeking ways to establish the Kingdom of God on earth before Rushdoony's time. My book does not address this longer history of dominion *ideas* in 20th-century America, where echoes are found, for example, in the writings of John Alexander Dowie, the founder of Zion City, Illinois. In March 1902, Dowie explained that "Zion City was founded and is being built for the purpose of the extension of the Kingdom of God upon earth. It is to this end that it is made a City where God shall rule in every department of family, industry, commercial, educational, ecclesiastical, and political life."[42] This political vision eventually came to be referred to as "dominion,"[43] which remains, in my estimation, the best descriptor to understand the quest for political power of Trump's evangelical supporters. In my book, I opt to use the politico-theological language of adherents instead of other popular labels. The most common term currently used is "Christian nationalism"; other labels are "Christo-fascism" and "Christian supremacy." In the case of "Christian nationalism," this sociological category has now been co-opted by so-called Christian nationalists, who gleefully use this designation to their own benefit. What was seemingly to be a sociological tool to analyze the social world of politically involved Christians has been co-opted and instrumentalized by social actors themselves and is now used to form political collectives of "insiders" and "outsiders."[44] Focusing instead on *theological concepts that originate from adherents themselves* helps to avoid some of the pitfalls of label re-appropriation for other means.[45]

As for one of the end-time views embraced by some NCPs, that of victorious eschatology, Wagner linked it to dominion theology.[46] But there are clearly other streams of influence, especially when dominion and eschatology are coupled with spiritual warfare. The triumphalist and spiritual warfare language used by some Christians can be traced back to the 1948 New Order of the Latter Rain (NOLR), and possibly even earlier. Some leaders of the movement anticipated the unveiling of the "Manifest Sons of God" in Romans 8.19–21. It was believed that the "Manifest Sons of God"—also referred to as the "Man-Child" (Revelation 12.5)[47]—were a supernaturally endowed Christian remnant to appear in the end-time NOLR revival. These "Overcomers" were now forming the corporal "Body of Christ" on earth and would come to possess the Kingdom of God. They would eventually rule and reign with Christ over the nations upon his return to earth (Revelation 3.26–27; 12.5).[48]

The corporal presence of Christ in the world through an end-time remnant is key to understanding this type of dominion. This feature, which was greatly accentuated in Earl Paulk's Kingdom Now teaching,[49] means that Christ must first return *into* the Church (through the members of his body) before returning *for* the Church. According to Paulk, "Christ in us must take dominion over the earth ... . The next move of God cannot occur until Christ in us takes dominion."[50] The way dominion will be taken echoes what was expected from the NOLR's "Manifest Sons of God," who were to rule over the nations. Paulk viewed the end-times harvest and the establishment of God's Kingdom in these terms:

> We are the ongoing incarnation of Christ who sow and reap spiritual seed ... Two kingdoms are in continuous conflict. The kingdom of darkness opposes the kingdom of light; the sons of the enemy battle the sons of the Kingdom. I proclaim to you that we have come to the time of the harvest, the end of the age. The gospel of the Kingdom will separate those who practice lawlessness from those whose witness will shine like the sun ... The book of Revelation makes it clear that John wrote his letters to the angels of the Church. Who are the angels that God will use? They are ministers called by God to boldly proclaim the Word of God. They will sound the trumpet ... Today the trumpet sounds from the angels of the Church. God's ministers who cry out, 'It is harvest time!' Witnesses to God's power will shine as never before. God will gather righteous people together to raise up a witness of Jesus Christ and judge the kingdoms of this world.[51]

Here is where the emphasis on the five-fold ministry (apostles, prophets, evangelists, pastors, and teachers; see Ephesians 4.11) comes into play,[52] since it is necessary to "equip the saints (Christians) for the work of ministry, for the edifying of the body of Christ, till we all come to the unity of the faith and of the knowledge of the Son of God, *to a perfect man*, to the measure of the stature of the fullness of Christ" (Ephesians 4.12–13). Bill Hamon[53] also clearly expressed this perspective:

> There can be no second coming until there is a full restoration of all things spoken by the prophets ... We make ready a people by transforming every saint into the image and likeness of Jesus so that they can manifest Christ's full manhood and ministry (Rom. 8:29). Present-day fivefold ministers and saints must accept the reality that there are things that the last generation of the mortal Church must fulfill and accomplish before Christ can return ... While Jesus was on earth, His natural body was the home and headquarters of God here on earth (Col. 2:9). Now the Church, as the corporate Body of Christ, is the home and headquarters for Jesus Christ here on earth (1 Cor. 12.27; Eph. 2.22) ... The twenty-first-century Church has a destiny to fulfill prophetic Scriptures just as Jesus fulfilled prophecies. There are many Old and New Testament prophetic Scriptures yet to be fulfilled by the Church. The mortal Church must fulfill all Scriptures pertaining to God's purpose for the last-generation Church

before Jesus can return. Therefore, it is *necessary for us to understand those prophetic Scriptures that must be restored and activated into reality before Jesus can be released from Heaven.*[54]

This expression of dominion differs considerably from that of Christian Reconstruction[55] which is why it often goes unnoticed. It is commonly assumed that NCPs just fashioned their dominion theology from Rushdoony's teachings, which is partly correct, but the supernaturalism of Charismatic dominion took root elsewhere. This type of dominion is not strictly a quest for U.S. societal transformation—it is global in nature.[56]

Issues of Biblical Interpretation

The interpretations of biblical texts as discussed in this book are those of NCP Trump-supporting leaders. These leaders are often unwilling to anchor their reading of the Bible according to more traditional Christian interpretations, and even less so on scholarly exegesis.[57] I have regrettably noticed that most of these leaders have little to no formal training in biblical exegesis and Christian theology[58] which is why there is clearly an interpretive conflict between the NCP reading of the Bible and that of more traditional and established churches.

NCPs see the Bible as a transhistorical text, where little attention is given to the context in which a text was produced. For example, when referring to the famous spiritual warfare text of Ephesians 6.12,[59] NCP leaders apply this biblical passage to their current socio-political struggle, without acknowledging nor understanding the context in which it was written. The 1st-century worldview of the early Christians at the time of the Roman Empire is not explained. Rather, these NCP leaders reread all texts related to spiritual opposition in light of their own political context. They must wage a "spiritual battle" against their enemy *now*. But the enemy is not the Roman Empire; rather, it all those who are under demonic control in this time and all around the world, opposing their religious freedom and the re-election of Donald Trump.

The Bible, as the Word of God, is also understood by many evangelicals to be inerrant, free from all error.[60] The very idea of "interpretation" is problematic and can sometimes be repugnant for some of these leaders, since it is believed that one can understand the message by simply reading the text. Most NCP leaders do not appeal to the long history of Christian interpretation;[61] the true meaning of Scripture is understood through the guidance of the Holy Spirit.[62] When reading my discussion about the various ways NCP Trump-supporting leaders use the Bible to legitimize their views on politics, church leadership and governance, spiritual warfare, eschatology, and a host of other issues, one must keep in mind that many of their proposed readings are not normative among Christians. The NCPs' use of the Bible in support of their political aspirations is clearly insufficient and lacks careful exegesis.[63]

Acknowledgments

In concluding this lengthy preface, I would like to acknowledge several colleagues who made this project possible. I wish to thank Philippe Gonzalez and Yannick Fer for believing in my work and inviting me to publish in *Enquêtes*. I greatly benefitted from their editorial remarks which clearly enriched my work. I am also indebted to my friend and colleague Philippe Gonzalez who has been a great conversation partner throughout the entire writing process and even afterward. Many of his insights have prevented this work from steering in the wrong direction; I am forever grateful for his keen analysis and precious suggestions. I also wish to thank Matthieu Megevand, Muriel Fullemann, and Michel Grandjean at Labor et Fides for their assistance in working out publication details for the translation with Routledge. A special thanks to Ceri McLardy, senior editor at Routledge, who has skillfully and patiently brokered the agreement with Labor et Fides. Thank you to Rebecca Clintworth, current publisher of Routledge Religion, Iman Hakimi, editorial assistant of Routledge Religion, for finalizing this publication, and Manmohan Negi and his team for the copyediting work.

This book would also not have been published without the support of Frances Flannery, who persistently sought out a publisher, believing that the American public and English-speaking world needed this work to be accessible. I want to extend my gratitude to Linda Shanahan who took it upon herself to voluntarily translate the entire French edition![64] I had not considered a possible English translation of my book before Linda contacted me to share her willingness to engage in such a demanding project. She deserves all the credit for making this project a reality. I end this list thanking Frederick Clarkson, Rachel Tabachnick, Bruce Wilson, Ruth Marshall,[65] and Elle Hardy[66] for all the fruitful discussions we had on the Christian Right, the New Apostolic Reformation, and Global Pentecostalism. On behalf of those involved in making it happen, I hope you all enjoy the book!

Notes

1 This translation also contains minor revisions and updates to the original text.
2 *Enquêtes* (Inquiries) is a book series which focuses on field or historical surveys mainly from a social science perspective. It is co-directed by Yannick Fer and Philippe Gonzalez.
3 Labor et Fides is a French Protestant publishing house located in Geneva, Switzerland.
4 Philippe Gonzalez is Senior Lecturer at l'Université de Lausanne (Switzerland) in the Faculty of Social and Political Sciences. Yannick Fer is a CNRS research director (Centre national de la recherche scientifique) in Paris, France.

5 The following are just a few examples—many more are not mentioned—of the plethora of books written on various issues concerning evangelicals during the Trump era.

6 Nelson (2019).

7 Stewart (2019); Whitehead and Perry (2020); Brockschmidt (2021); Gorski and Perry (2022); Onishi (2023).

8 Du Mez (2020).

9 Barr (2021).

10 Compton (2020); Posner (2020).

11 Tisby (2019); Jones (2020); Butler (2021).

12 See the Introduction for my definition of NCPs.

13 Juergensmeyer and Kanwal Sheikh (2013, p. 626) define the sociotheological approach as one which understands that "religion is related to other aspects of society, from economic and political factors to matters of social identity ... religion can account for social phenomena and social factors can account for religion."

14 Digital ethnography is comprised of "data-gathering methods [that] are mediated by computer-mediated communication" which includes "digitally mediated field-notes, online participant observation, blogs/wikis with contributions by respondents, and online focus groups and can also include accounts of offline groups" (Pink et al. 2016, p. 5).

15 The aim of discourse analysis, according to Norman Fairclough (1995, p. 132), is "to systematically explore often opaque relationships of causality and determination between (a) discursive practices, events and texts, and (b) wider social and cultural structures, relations and processes; to investigate how such practices, events and texts arise out of and are ideologically shaped by relations of power and struggles over power."

16 My primary sources were books, articles, transcripts, blogs, podcasts, videos, and other audio segments.

17 Meyer (2010, pp. 116–117).

18 In his new book on the New Apostolic Reformation, Trump and evangelical politics, Damon T. Berry (2023) mentions the 2020 French edition of my book and covers similar themes.

19 I mention, however, the specter of civil war in Chapter 3. For more on the political theology of power that inspired some to participate in the January 6, 2021, Capitol insurrection, see also Gagné (2023). The brewing feeling of civil war in the United States was recently documented by Jeff Sharlet (2023). A podcast series written by Matthew D. Taylor and aired on the Straight White American Jesus podcast highlights the influence of several New Apostolic Reformation leaders in the January 6th insurrection; see https://icjs.org/charismatic-revival-fury/ (accessed 29 May 2023). See also Taylor and Onishi's article in *Religion Dispatches*: https://religiondispatches.org/evidence-strongly-suggests-trump-was-collaborating-with-christian-nationalist-leaders-before-january-6th/ (accessed 29 May 2023).

20 Frederick Clarkson and I wrote about a rift in the New Apostolic Reformation (NAR) movement in *Religion Dispatches*: https://religiondispatches.org/new-apostolic-reformation-faces-profound-rift-due-to-trump-prophecies-and-spiritual-manipulation-of-the-prophetic-gift/ (accessed 12 December 2022).

21 See Stewart (2014) and Anderson (2007; 2013).

22 For example, as reported by the Irvingites in the early 19th century CE, see Strachan (1973) and Robinson (2011).

23 There have been a number of books written on the NAR by Christian apologists, such as Pivec and Geivett (2022).

24 See Wagner (2004, p. 12).

25 Cook edited a defining five-volume anthology on apostleship entitled *Aligning with the Apostolic*, featuring prominent apostles such as Tim Hamon, Robert Henderson, Bill Johnson, Rick Joyner, and Joseph Mattera, to name a few. C. Peter Wagner, Lance Wallnau, Johnny Enlow, and Bill Hamon are among the other significant leaders to have written a foreword to one of the five volumes; see Cook (2013).
26 Wagner (2013a, p. xxvi).
27 Wagner (2013a, p. xxvi); emphasis mine.
28 Wagner (2013a, p. xxvii).
29 Wagner wrote in another foreword (Wagner 2013b, p. 2) to a book on Apostolic Centers, "Focusing for the moment on my home territory of North America, my best estimate is that the second apostolic age began here in 2001. That is when we reached a critical mass of churches moving into apostolic government, from which there will be no turning back."
30 For Wagner, the NAR is "the process of change in the Church" which he traced back to 1900, whereas the Second Apostolic Age "is a historical season, not a process." It is the result of the NAR process which began in the early 20th century; see Wagner (2004, p. 12).
31 See Wagner (1998, p. 18).
32 Mattera (2022, p. 65).
33 For more on Willow Creek Community Church, see https://www.willowcreek.org (accessed 27 May 2023).
34 See Wagner (1999, p. 40).
35 Wagner (1999, p. 35).
36 Wagner (2000a, p. 25).
37 Wagner (1999, p. 179).
38 Wagner (1999, p. 219).
39 Wagner (1999; see dedication).
40 Jackson (1999, p. 367).
41 See Chapter 1 for my discussion of dominion theology.
42 See Dowie, *Leaves of Healing*, Vol 11.2, May 3, 1902, p. 66.
43 While often referred to as "dominionism," the term used by its advocates is "dominion" or "dominion theology."
44 I wish to thank Philippe Gonzalez for his insight on this issue.
45 Some will nonetheless try to redefine what is meant by "dominionism." A case in point is Johnny Enlow, who has reframed dominionism saying "it is no more or less than Jesus' original assignment of 'You are salt of the earth,' and 'You are the light of the world.'" Those who have read Enlow's three books on the "7 Mountain Mandate" will beg to differ; see https://www.instagram.com/p/CnAYBqLJthb/?igshid=YmMyMTA2M2Y%3D (accessed 27 May 2023).
46 See Chapter 4 for my discussion of the various eschatological views held by evangelicals and their political implications.
47 The NOLR was not the first movement to use expressions such as "Man-Child" or "Overcomers" to designate a select group of end-time believers. Early Pentecostals such as Charles Parham used these terms to describe an end-time remnant selected from the Bride of Christ (the Church); see Parham (1902, p. 86).
48 For more on the specific references to NOLR teachings, see Faupel (2010, pp. 253–255).
49 Bishop Earl Paulk (1927–2009) was an American pastor and co-founder of a former megachurch in Atlanta, Georgia called Chapel Hill Harvester Church (it is now Spirit and Truth Sanctuary); for more information, see http://www.mytruthsanctuary.com/aboutus_history.html (accessed 8 January 2023).
50 See Paulk (1985, p. 234).

51 Paulk (1986, pp. 103–104).
52 The restoration of apostles and prophets, for example, is not something new. Early Pentecostal pioneers such as W. F. Carothers, one of Charles Parham's assistants, wrote in 1909 about the role of apostles and prophets in the government of the church; see Faupel (2010, p. 39).
53 Bill Hamon is the founder of Christian International Ministries and is referred to as the father of the Prophetic Movement; see https://christianinternational.com/about/dr-bill-hamons-story/ (accessed 27 May 2023).
54 See Hamon (2021, pp. 287; 289; 293–294).
55 For more on Christian Reconstruction, see Chapter 1.
56 See Clarkson and Gagné https://religiondispatches.org/when-it-comes-to-societal-dominion-the-details-matter-a-reporters-guide-to-the-new-apostolic-reformation-part-ii/ (accessed 27 May 2023).
57 A must read for those who wish to know what the Bible really says according to biblical scholarship on various socio-political issues such as climate change, poverty, education, sexuality, abortion, immigration, gay rights, and government, see Flannery, Frances, and Rodney Alan Werline, eds. *The Bible in Political Debate: What Does It Really Say?* London: Bloomsbury T&T Clark, 2016.
58 By formal training, I mean with an accredited post-secondary institution such as a Theology or Religious Studies department in a university.
59 "For we do not wrestle against flesh and blood, but against principalities, against powers, against the rulers of the darkness of this age, against spiritual *hosts* of wickedness in the heavenly places."
60 Most would hold the view of the Bible as expressed in the Chicago Statement on Biblical Inerrancy and Hermeneutics; see https://defendinginerrancy.com/chicago-statements/ (accessed 27 May 2023).
61 For a thorough review of the history of biblical interpretation, see Henning Graf Reventlow's masterful four-volume work, *History of Biblical Interpretation* (SBL Resources for Biblical Studies 50, 61, 62, 63). Atlanta: Society of Biblical Literature, 2009, 2010.
62 Some like to quote 1 John 2.27 in support of their view: "As for you, the anointing you received from him remains in you, and you do not need anyone to teach you. But as his anointing teaches you about all things …"
63 For more on how the Bible is sometimes rewritten for political purposes, see Kiddie (2020).
64 Excepting the preface, updates, and epilogue, which I have written in English for the Routledge edition.
65 See Marshall's insightful work on Pentecostalism and politics in Nigeria (2009).
66 I had many discussions with Elle Hardy about Pentecostalism; see her recent book on Global Pentecostalism (2022).

INTRODUCTION

Donald Trump garnered the unfailing support of millions of American evangelicals. According to some, the American president was understood to be "chosen by God,"[1] was a "new Messiah,"[2] and was even compared to Jesus by one Republican senator![3] One is compelled to question who these evangelicals are and what they believe. Who are their most influential leaders, and what plans do they have for social and political transformation? (It should be noted from the outset that not all "evangelicals" share the same beliefs, nor do they all back President Trump.)

This book focuses on a specific strand of American evangelicalism, one which is currently having a profound impact in the United States and globally. Our attention will primarily be on "Charismatic" evangelicals, although at times we will also refer to other evangelical groups with whom they share common ideas or have points of disagreement.

White evangelical "born again"[4] Christians played a significant role in the 2016 U.S. presidential election:[5] 81% voted in favor of Donald J. Trump.[6] But it was during the 2018 midterm elections that Trump received his greatest support from White Christians, bringing in 75% of evangelical voters, 56% of Protestants, and 49% of Catholics. Fifty-four percent of the White Christian vote went to Republican candidates, whereas only 9% of African Americans, 29% of Latino Americans, and 23% of Asian Americans voted for Republicans.[7]

Who Are Evangelicals?

Scholars are still struggling with how to define the term "evangelical."[8] Is it a religious movement? A pastor would certainly acknowledge as much. In the

DOI: 10.4324/9781003358718-1

context of certain Christian communities, "evangelical" characterizes someone who is "born again." But prominent evangelical figures in the United States have made this religious movement a central part of American politics. According to some commentators,[9] evangelicalism has even infiltrated and taken control of the Republican Party, to the extent that, for an American politician, "evangelical" has become virtually synonymous with "White, Christian, and Republican."

The word "evangelical" derives from "evangel," meaning gospel, or "good news," and can describe an individual, Church, or organization specifically proclaiming the news of Jesus Christ as savior of the world.[10] This definition is too broad, however, as it also characterizes the activism of some religious groups that do not consider themselves part of evangelicalism (Catholics, Mormons, Jehovah's Witnesses, etc.). Historian David Bebbington identifies four characteristics which, according to him, define the "evangelical" movement:[11] (1) Conversion—the experience of a "new birth"; (2) Biblicism—the Bible as the foundation of faith; (3) Crucicentrism—the centrality of Jesus' crucifixion and its saving effects; and (4) Activism—evangelical proselytizing and social action. Sociologist Philippe Gonzalez rightly notes that Bebbington's taxonomy has proved helpful for researchers and was even used by evangelicals to legitimize their place in society.[12] However, Gonzalez points out that despite its usefulness, this definition, which focuses on specific characteristics, fails to recognize the significance of evangelicalism as a social movement.

The contemporary meaning of the words "evangelical" or "evangelicalism" was established in the 1940s as the result of efforts carried out by neo-evangelical leaders of the time, who wished to breathe new life into a conservative American Protestantism profoundly discredited by the effects of fundamentalism at the beginning of the 20th century.[13] These neo-evangelical leaders produced a more palatable narrative regarding their "evangelical" identity, claiming it to be very old and even harkening back to the 16th-century Reformation.[14] This newly devised narrative—insistently presented as normative—was then taken up by historians, sociologists, and statisticians, without subjecting it to rigorous and critical investigation. However, such a re-working of ancient history has very problematic repercussions regarding diversity within conservative Protestant movements. It forces a monolithic identity with little consideration for the historical, theological, and liturgical differences between diverse groups (Baptists, Methodists, Presbyterians, etc.). All these various factions would now be reduced to the simple label of "evangelical," even if the National Association of Evangelicals (founded in 1942 and representing some 45,000 churches from more than forty denominations)[15] recognized that:

> Evangelicals are a vibrant and diverse group, including believers found in many churches, denominations and nations. Our community brings

together Reformed, Holiness, Anabaptist, Pentecostal, Charismatic and other traditions.[16]

These early neo-evangelical leaders thus succeeded in uniting most Protestant groups[17] under the same banner and set of conservative beliefs. This coalition was also necessary for the battle they sought to wage against the sort of "theological liberalism" promoted by another wing of Protestantism. A more liberal strain of Protestantism professed that the Bible and Christian dogmas should be subject to scientific inquiry, like all other human constructs, and could therefore be critiqued and relativized. This battle against theological liberalism went hand in hand with a war against a liberal society and its mores. Today, evangelicalism is a large coalition which has captured national attention in the United States since its arrival into politics in the 1980s.[18]

The evangelical faction which supported President Trump is part of the Christian right, a religious coalition with political aspirations. They stand against a pluralistic society, notably on moral issues, but also on religious ones, and their goal is to impose a "Judeo-Christian" hegemony on American society. While comprised primarily of evangelicals, this politico-religious movement also brings together Catholics and ultra-conservative Protestants. This seemingly diverse coalition is centered around common causes[19] such as anti-abortion activism, opposition to the rights of LGBTQ+ citizens and to sexual education courses, promotion of prayer and the teaching of creationism (or of "intelligent design") in public schools, and the safeguard of their religious freedom.[20] The goal of the Christian right is essentially this: to impose Christian nationalism[21] wherein "Judeo-Christian values" are fundamentally the laws of the land.[22] With that in mind, this book focuses specifically on the sociopolitical impact of one important evangelical group: Charismatics who supported Donald Trump.

Charismatic Roots

Contemporary Charismatics have their roots in a 17th-century Protestant movement known as pietism, a branch founded by Lutheran pastor Philipp Jacob Spener, which stressed piety and religious sentiment over doctrinal knowledge.[23] A century later, John Wesley, an Anglican Church minister, was to make significant contributions to this Protestant tradition. Wesley traveled throughout England preaching revival in the form of mass conversions to a Christian faith, which was to be actively chosen and practiced, rather than the staid cultural varnish of an inherited Christian religion. He launched the Methodist movement, the term designating in part—ironically—the rigorous "method" converts used to put into practice their devotion and achieve a disciplined life.

Concurrently, on the North American continent, the First Great Awakening (1730–1755) was taking place under the influence of preachers and revivalists Jonathan Edwards and George Whitefield. This movement was later followed by the Second Great Awakening (1790–1840), led by Charles Grandison Finney, called the "father of modern revivalism" of the 19th century.[24] Following the Protestant pietistic example, these revival movements stressed the profound sentiments of piety which must, according to the revivalists, accompany the conversion experience.

In addition, another pivotal element emerging from the history of American Protestantism should be noted: that of revivalist Phoebe Palmer and the Holiness Movement.[25] In 1837, Palmer began teaching that the "baptism of the Holy Spirit" instantly produces a life of full holiness and removes all sinful tendencies in believers, a process which is called "sanctification." This idea will pave the way for the Pentecostal movement.

Near the end of the 19th century, a small group of the faithful met in a Bible school in Topeka, Kansas. Led by Charles Fox Parham, a preacher with a Methodist background, the group studied the accounts of miracles in the New Testament. The participants were particularly struck by the story of the Pentecost in the book of Acts, where those who were baptized in the Holy Spirit "began to speak in other tongues" (*NIV*, Acts 2.4). Legend has it that on January 1, 1901, during a time of prayer and fasting, a student named Agnes Ozman began to "speak in other tongues." Parham and the other students had the same experience some days later. According to Parham, the baptism in the Holy Spirit must always be accompanied by speaking in tongues.[26] He claimed this phenomenon to be a distinct experience from that of conversion and sanctification. By 1906, the Pentecostal awakening had reached Los Angeles, California. It was there, in a small church on Azusa Street, that many received the baptism of the Spirit and began to speak in tongues.[27] This happened under the leadership of African American preacher William J. Seymour. Seymour had also been associated with the Holiness Movement, having studied under Parham.

Parham and Seymour believed that speaking in tongues was a sign of the "end times." These "foreign languages" were understood to be a gift to missionaries allowing them to evangelize people whose language they did not know. Missionaries would be sent to nations that had not yet heard the Gospel, to preach the message of salvation before the return of Christ.[28] For these Christians, this spectacular gift of the Spirit was closely linked to the imminent end of the world.

Pentecostalism has a complex history stemming from 17th-century pietism with influences spanning from Wesley and the two Great Awakenings of the 18th and 19th centuries—led by Edwards, Whitefield, and Finney—to the Holiness Movement marked by figures such as Palmer, Parham, and Seymour.

We will now see how these roots have led us to the current form of Charismatic Christianity.

The Three "Waves of the Spirit" and Their Deep Influence

The brand of Charismatic Christianity we examine in this book is the product of a historical trajectory which began just over 100 years ago. In Charismatic and Pentecostal circles, people often refer to "three waves of the Spirit"[29] which are, in fact, three periods in the history of contemporary Charismatic Christianity where the "Pentecostal experience" extended to other Christian movements. The "first wave of the Spirit" coincides with the birth of Pentecostalism at the turn of the 20th century. This wave had a considerable impact on a movement known as the "New Order of the Latter Rain" in the late 1940s.[30] Tension occurred when institutional authorities (church officials and ecclesial bodies) within Pentecostalism denounced this new movement. The New Order of the Latter Rain originated in the small city of North Battleford, Saskatchewan, Canada,[31] in 1948. The revival held in the small North Battleford Sharon Bible School was strongly discredited and disapproved of by some churches of the time.[32] The Assemblies of God, for example, issued a resolution condemning some of the beliefs and practices of the Latter Rain.[33] Among the grievances mentioned[34] was the idea that "gifts of the Spirit" are identified, transferred, confirmed, or conferred through the laying on of hands and a prophetic word. They also opposed the claim that prophetic inspiration could serve as a prescriptive guide for individuals' lives. The idea that the Church was to be built on the teaching of contemporary "apostles" and "prophets" was also rejected.[35] Despite the reluctance and disavowal of the most important Pentecostal churches at the time, the Latter Rain revival had a global impact. Its influence is still felt in contemporary Pentecostalism[36] and among Charismatics who supported Trump.

The "Pentecostal experience" was followed by a "second wave of the Spirit" in the 1960s.[37] It was a time of "Charismatic renewal," with manifestations of the Spirit[38] spreading to traditional churches. Major Protestant denominations—Anglicans, Presbyterians, Lutherans, Methodists—experienced this phenomenon. It even extended its reach to Roman Catholics, creating one of the most powerful Catholic movements at the end of Vatican II. The Charismatic renewal would serve as arbiter between progressives and conservatives, emphasizing a particularly strong allegiance to papal authority.

Another important contribution of the "second wave of the Spirit" was the Shepherding/Discipleship Movement, which emerged in the late 1970s. The ecumenism that resulted from the Charismatic renewal was seen by some as too chaotic. Roman Catholic leaders, in particular, felt that it brought Charismatic Catholics dangerously close to Protestantism. The Shepherding/Discipleship Movement came as a response to such concerns.

Leaders associated with the Shepherding Movement taught that each believer had to submit to a spiritual authority—placing oneself "under the cover" or protection—of a "shepherd," i.e., a spiritual leader from a local church.[39] This shepherd was responsible not only for the spiritual well-being of those placed under his authority, but also for ensuring their emotional, educational, financial, professional, and social development. In agreeing to submit to a shepherd, the faithful recognized the authority of those whom God chose to watch over them, a recognition requiring great transparency and even an openness to reproof when necessary.[40] The Shepherding Movement officially came to an end in the mid-1980s.[41] We will see how the ecclesial structure proposed by this movement—and strongly inspired by the Latter Rain—still serves as a model for a certain faction of the Charismatic movement today.

The expression "third wave" was coined by C. Peter Wagner (1930–2016), missiologist, Church growth specialist, and the main leader of the New Apostolic Reformation.[42] The "third wave of the Spirit" is said by Wagner to have occurred at the beginning of the 1980s. This wave reached evangelicals who were not affected by the first two "waves," either Pentecostalism or the Charismatic renewal. This new wave differed from Pentecostalism in its interpretation regarding the "baptism in the Holy Spirit."[43] Traditional Pentecostals mainly believe that speaking in tongues is the initial sign of the "baptism of the Spirit." However, "third wave" Charismatics do not believe that speaking in tongues is given to everyone, nor is it the sign of the Spirit's baptism. They consider "tongues" to be just *one* of many spiritual gifts.

John Wimber (1934–1997), leader of the Vineyard Movement in the 1980s and 1990s, played a determining role in the emergence of this "third wave." C. Peter Wagner and John Wimber first met in the mid-1970s. However, it wasn't until 1982 that Wagner invited Wimber to teach a course at Fuller Theological Seminary[44] called "MC510 *Signs, Wonders and Church Growth*." Wimber taught the course from 1982 to 1985 and included a practical workshop during the last hour of class where he demonstrated the "gifts of the Spirit." Despite the controversy among the Fuller Seminary faculty, many participants testified to healings, including Wagner himself, and to "words of knowledge" received from Wimber.[45] In Pentecostal and Charismatic circles, a "word of knowledge" is understood to be an immediate and specific supernatural "revelation" given by God to an individual for the benefit of one person or one church. Such a revelation could be related to a sickness and the promise of healing, or to the disclosure of an unknown problem and of a forthcoming solution, etc. These "signs, wonders and miracles" are also associated with "power evangelism," where the proclamation of the Christian message and its truth is demonstrated through supernatural means. This is one of the characteristics of the "third wave" initiated by Wimber's ministry.[46]

At the end of the 1980s, Wagner pursued his missiological research on the root causes of the phenomenal growth taking place in Pentecostal and Charismatic churches around the world. He was led to explore two areas which were to wield considerable influence on the actual form of the Charismatic movement and its contemporary impact: spiritual warfare[47] and the New Apostolic Reformation.[48] Wagner taught that believers take part in a spiritual war between good and evil, where demonic forces battle against Christians. We will return to this idea in Chapter 3. As an idea of neo-charismatic influence, the New Apostolic Reformation is closely related to the "third wave." Wagner believed that the New Apostolic Reformation's influence in American churches was linked to a historical season which he called "the Second Apostolic Age" in 2001. Chapters 2 and 3 are dedicated to some of the characteristics of this movement which seeks to restore the strategic role of apostles in church life. The New Apostolic Reformation incorporated many of the beliefs and practices of Pentecostals and Charismatics, which have been present in Charismatic Christianity in the United States for over a century. This movement seeks to establish a new form of church governance—which it claims to be historically more valid—and recasts the church's role in society. This will lead us to the political role that the New Apostolic Reformation takes on—no less than the sociopolitical transformation of nations with the goal of bringing about the Kingdom of God on earth.

The Charismatic Quest for Political Power

For some of the Charismatics close to the seats of political power, President Trump represented the only hope for the United States. As we will see in Chapter 1, he has in fact been compared to the Persian King Cyrus the Great, chosen by God to free the Jewish people from the grip of their captivity in the 6th century BCE. We will examine how the political interests of Charismatics who supported Trump have their roots in a theology of power, according to which Christians have a divine mandate to exercise dominion in the world, according to their interpretation of a text in the book of Genesis (*KJV*, Gen. 1.26–28). The plan to bring about social change is most often framed as that of conquering the "Seven Mountains" or cultural spheres of influence. These overlapping spheres encompass all aspects of daily life: religion, education, business, government, arts and entertainment, media, and the family.[49] The objective is to influence and control each of these "mountains" so as to establish the Kingdom of God on earth according to the Our Father prayer: "your kingdom come, your will be done, on earth as it is in heaven" (*NIV*, Matt. 6.10).

In Chapter 2 we will analyze how this social transformation strategy is to be carried out by contemporary "apostles" and their "apostolic centers," places devoted to training believers for their envisaged sociopolitical plan.

The ecclesial model of these apostolic centers differs considerably from that of traditional evangelical churches. The decision-making power which once rested on the community of believers is now in the hands of an apostle. We will see how these training centers are also linked to "apostolic networks"—comprised of various religious and political entrepreneurs, who are in the business of developing the "Seven Mountains" cultural strategy.

The hegemonic plan of these Charismatics is not free from opposition, of course, and in Chapter 3 we will see how any hindrance to Trump or to the advancement of their social transformation program was understood in terms of spiritual warfare. Beyond the spiritual battle lies the menace of a second American Civil War, because the former American president and the Christians who supported him shared common enemies. Hence, it comes as no surprise to see Paula White-Cain, Trump's White House spiritual counselor, deliver "warfare prayers" against the demonic forces, which are believed to be the attacks led by the Democrats against President Trump. By using the theological metaphor of spiritual warfare, she legitimized the demonization of Trump's political adversaries, ensuring that some proportion of evangelicals would continue to support the former president.

Since many of these Charismatic Trump supporters viewed him as God's chosen leader, some were also on the lookout for signs of the "end times," linking eschatology to his political actions. It is this connection that we will explore in Chapter 4. The relocation of the American embassy from Tel Aviv to Jerusalem in May 2018 and the Middle East peace plan were two such examples which galvanized Christian Zionists in America. According to an eschatological reading of certain biblical texts, the Jewish people must inhabit Abraham's "promised land" before the second coming of Christ, when he will then establish his thousand-year reign from Jerusalem. For some believers, the Iranian-American conflict, exacerbated by the assassination of Iranian general Qassem Soleimani on January 3, 2020, heralded an event preceding the "rapture" of the Church*[50] (NIV, 1 Thess. 4.13–18). Indeed, for some eschatological enthusiasts, Iran (formerly Persia) is one of the nations which will be part of a coalition led by Russia to attack the modern State of Israel in the last days, according to a futurist interpretation of the war of Gog and Magog (NIV, Ezek. 38–39). For some Christians enamored with eschatology, the assassination of Soleimani and the U.S. defense of Israel could lead to a future coalition of "Gog and Magog" against the Jewish state.

To summarize, the ideas of "dominion," "spiritual warfare," and "eschatology" are key beliefs among Charismatic Trump supporters. With the upcoming 2024 election, can we afford to overlook how these ideas have shaped politics under the Trump administration? Let's explore how these ideas have impacted some Charismatics who held positions of power in America during the Trump era.

Notes

1 See https://religionnews.com/2018/09/26/film-trump-prophecy-mark-taylor-gods-plan-liberty-university/ (accessed 22 May 2023).
2 See https://www.counterpunch.org/2019/11/29/when-trump-became-messiah-to-the-american-right/ (accessed 22 May 2023).
3 See https://time.com/5752453/trump-jesus-comparison-impeachment-debate/ (accessed 22 May 2023).
4 The expression "born again" is used by many evangelicals to describe their conversion experience.
5 For more on the mobilization strategies and digital influence of certain evangelical groups in the 2016 election, see Nelson (2019).
6 https://www.prri.org/spotlight/religion-vote-presidential-election-2004-2016/ (accessed 22 May 2023).
7 https://www.pewresearch.org/fact-tank/2019/03/18/evangelical-approval-of-trump-remains-high-but-other-religious-groups-are-less-supportive/ (accessed 22 May 2023).
8 See Dayton (1997) as well as Timothy Gloedge, "#ITSNOTUS: Being Evangelical Means Never Having To Say You're Sorry": https://religiondispatches.org/itsnotus-being-evangelical-means-never-having-to-say-youre-sorry/ (accessed 22 May 2023).
9 John Turner, "Evangelicalism: A Political Movement?": https://www.patheos.com/blogs/anxiousbench/2018/08/evangelicalism-a-political-movement/ (accessed 22 May 2023).
10 Jonathan Merritt, "Defining 'Evangelical'": https://www.theatlantic.com/politics/archive/2015/12/evangelical-christian/418236/ (accessed 22 May 2023).
11 See Bebbington (1989, pp. 2–17).
12 Gonzalez (2014, p. 30).
13 Gonzalez (2014, pp. 31–32).
14 Hart (2004, p. 38).
15 https://www.nae.net/about-nae/ (accessed 22 May 2023).
16 https://www.nae.net/what-is-an-evangelical/ (accessed 22 May 2023).
17 Hart (2004, p. 53).
18 Hart (2004, p. 176).
19 Concerning the political mobilization of the Christian right around ultra-conservative values in the United States, see Diamond (1990, 1995, 1998), Bruce (1988), Critchlow (2005), Balmer (2010), Williams (2010), and FitzGerald (2017).
20 Not to allow open opposition to the rights of LGBTQ+ people or opposing the teaching of creationism in schools would be a violation of their religious freedom. Their "integralist objection" argues that "political liberalism violates its own commitment to freedom, neutrality, and inclusion, by restricting the ability of citizens and public actors to appeal to their religious convictions in the political public space"; see Stavo-Debauge (2015, p. 172).
21 On the rise of Christian nationalism in the United States, see Stewart (2019) as well as Whitehead and Perry (2020).
22 See https://www.npr.org/2020/03/12/815097747/survey-most-evangelicals-see-trump-as-honest-and-morally-upstanding/ (accessed 22 May 2023).
23 Concerning Spener and the Protestant pietist movement, see Stoeffler (1971), Stein (1986), and Weborg (1997).
24 See Dayton and Strong (2014).
25 Bassett (1997).
26 Wacker (2001, pp. 5–6).
27 See Faupel (1996, pp. 14–15).

28 See Vinson Synan, "Pentecostal Millennialism: The Second Comers": https://christianhistoryinstitute.org/magazine/article/pentecostal-millennialism-the-second-comers/ (accessed 22 May 2023).

29 See Bartoş (2015).

30 Riss (1987, pp. 105–124).

31 Holdcroft explains that at that time George Hawtin, senior leader of New Order of the Latter Rain, had resigned in 1947 from the Pentecostal Assemblies of Canada following an administrative dispute. This conflict led him to take responsibility for the Sharon Orphanage and to undertake creation of a Bible school; see Holdcroft (1980).

32 For more details on the history of this movement and of its revival, see Riss (1987), Holdcroft (1980), Faupel (2010).

33 One can read the resolution in *Minutes of the Twenty-Third Council of the Assemblies of God* (1949, pp. 26–27).

34 See also the booklet *Assemblies of God – Heritage* (1987, p. 16).

35 We will return to the significance of "apostles" and "prophets" in the second chapter.

36 Hutchinson (2010).

37 On the rise of Charismatic Christianity and its impact in the 1960s; see Maiden (2023).

38 Gonzalez (2014, p. 39).

39 This movement was popularized by the Fort Lauderdale Five, a group of five leaders from Fort Lauderdale, Florida: Bob Mumford, Charles Simpson, Derek Prince, Don Basham, and Ern Baxter; see Moore (2003, pp. 33–45).

40 Moore (2003, p. 74).

41 See *Ministries Today* (January–February 1990, p. 52).

42 We will return to the New Apostolic Reformation, an important and influential faction associated to the "third wave."

43 Wagner (1988, pp. 18–19).

44 Fuller is an evangelical seminary in Pasadena, California. They host the largest missiology institute in the world.

45 Wagner published a report on the impact of the MC510 course at Fuller: Wagner (1987).

46 See Wimber (1985).

47 For more details on the history and origins of the contemporary movement dedicated to spiritual warfare and "spiritual mapping," see Holvast (2009).

48 On the history, beliefs, and practices of the New Apostolic Reformation, see Weaver (2016); Rachel Tabachnick, "The Ideology and History of the New Apostolic Reformation": http://www.talk2action.org/story/2011/8/12/1713/01915/; Bruce Wilson, "Burning Buddhas, Books, and Art: Meet The New Apostolic Reformation": http://www.talk2action.org/story/2011/9/14/192516/418/Front_Page/Burning_Buddhas_Books_and_Art_Meet_The_New_Apostolic_Reformation/ (accessed 22 May 2023).

49 There was recent shift which we will not explore in this book concerning the Seven Mountains. The main promoter of the "Seven Mountain Mandate" is Lance Wallnau. In December 2022 Wallnau explained that his mountain strategy went through a shift. Now, the arts, entertainment, and media have been grouped into a single cluster to make room for a new mountain: the science and technology mountain; see https://rumble.com/v221a40-announcing-a-brand-new-mountain.html (accessed 22 May 2023).

50 When it comes to the invisible universal Church, we add the asterisk (*) to distinguish between the Church as an institution and the church as a place.

1

THE NEW CYRUS AND THE "SEVEN MOUNTAINS" OF CULTURE

During a January 3, 2020, meeting of the "evangelicals for Trump" coalition in Miami, Apostle Guillermo Maldonado asked God for the president to be a "Cyrus," to bring about reformation, and for all nations to recognize America as the greatest nation on earth.[1] Who is "Cyrus," and where does the idea originate that Donald J. Trump is comparable to this biblical figure?

A few months before Trump's election to the presidency of the United States in 2016, Lance Wallnau published *God's Chaos Candidate: Donald J. Trump and the American Unraveling*. Wallnau is a Pentecostal Christian businessman, who is also regarded as a prophet, an apostle, and a teacher. His website describes him as follows:

> … a strategist, futurist and compelling communicator who has shared platforms with Ben Carson, Mike Pompeo, and best-selling authors Ken Blanchard and John Maxwell. He has conducted training for the United Nations and spoken at Harvard, the Chinese Academy of Social Sciences, and the London School of Theology. With a thirty-year background consulting business and non-profits, Lance's students represent a global tapestry spanning governments, CEOs, entertainers, and entrepreneurs.[2]

Wallnau alludes to his connections with two Republican politicians, who were both members of the Trump administration: Ben Carson, a retired pediatric neurosurgeon who was a Republican candidate for the presidency in 2016, and who became Secretary of Housing and Urban Development, and Mike Pompeo, the former American Secretary of State. Wallnau then mentions Blanchard and Maxwell, two American authors, business

DOI: 10.4324/9781003358718-2

consultants, and specialists in leadership training and development. This brief biographical sketch makes it clear that Wallnau prides himself in his associations with the world's powerful and in his influence on them.

As a young adult, Wallnau studied at Valley Forge Military Academy and College in Pennsylvania, where he claimed to have had a conversion experience. After graduating from VFMA in 1973, Wallnau enrolled at Oral Roberts University (ORU) in Oklahoma.[3] Following a discussion with a theology student, Wallnau realized that his conversion experience at the Military Academy was a "new birth." The expression "new birth" or "to be born again" is a term frequently used by evangelicals to describe the conversion experience leading to salvation.[4] This experience represents a new start for the believer, where they shed their past life to become a follower of Christ. Some Christian groups require their members to be baptized by immersion after having made a profession of faith to Christ in obedience to Jesus' command in Matthew 28.19, enjoining the disciples to baptize new believers.[5] Not long after, Wallnau was baptized by immersion and received the Spirit's baptism.[6]

Wallnau claims to have obtained a master's degree at Southwestern Christian University, where he then taught for a while, followed by a Doctor of Ministry degree—a graduate degree in pastoral ministry—at the Phoenix University of Theology.[7] For 20 years, Wallnau worked as both a pastor and a business executive in the oil industry. Since the year 2000, he has solely focused on consulting in the business world because he believes this is where God has called him to work.[8]

Wallnau was the first to promote the idea that Trump was God's chosen one, comparable to Cyrus the Great, King of Persia. He even predicted Trump's victory six months before the election. He recounted how God revealed to him that Trump would be a "wrecking ball" against the spirit of "political correctness."[9] God had also confided to Wallnau that the biblical reference of Isaiah 45 corresponded to Donald Trump's providential mission as 45th president of the United States. This biblical chapter concerns the mission of the Persian King Cyrus. Donald Trump would be a contemporary incarnation of this figure:

> 44^{28} [I am the LORD] who says of Cyrus, 'He is my shepherd
>   and will accomplish all that I please;
> he will say of Jerusalem, "Let it be rebuilt,"
>   and of the temple, "Let its foundations be laid."'
>
> 45^1 "This is what the LORD says to his anointed,
>   to Cyrus, whose right hand I take hold of
> to subdue nations before him
>   and to strip kings of their armor,

to open doors before him
  so that gates will not be shut:
²I will go before you
  and will level the mountains;
I will break down gates of bronze
  and cut through bars of iron.
³I will give you hidden treasures,
  riches stored in secret places,
so that you may know that I am the LORD,
  the God of Israel, who summons you by name.
⁴For the sake of Jacob my servant,
  of Israel my chosen,
I summon you by name
  and bestow on you a title of honor,
  though you do not acknowledge me....

¹³I will raise up Cyrus in my righteousness:
  I will make all his ways straight.
He will rebuild my city
  and set my exiles free,
but not for a price or reward,
  says the LORD Almighty."

Isaiah 44.28; 45.1–4.13[10]

Although Cyrus was a pagan king, he is nonetheless called "messiah of the Lord," i.e., God's chosen one.[11] Likewise, Trump's evangelical supporters did not hesitate to characterize him as "Chosen by God," a title which Trump gladly appropriated for himself. During a press conference on August 21, 2019, to defend his trade war against China, Trump presented himself as "the chosen one," something which the mainstream media did not fail to notice.[12]

Of course, there is no need to be a perfect example of charity and Christian morality to be "God's chosen one." Even some of Trump's Charismatic supporters would assert that God could use flawed individuals—Cyrus being just one example. According to the biblical narrative, the Persian King invaded Babylon in 539 BCE, freed the Jews, and offered them generous donations so they could reconstruct their temple in Jerusalem.[13] Even as he was lauded by the prophet Isaiah as the liberating "shepherd" of God's chosen people, Cyrus remained a pagan king who honored other gods such as Marduk (Babylonia), Baal (Phenicia), and Mazda (Persia). King Cyrus, like Trump, was rich, powerful, and pagan—and had nothing in common with the faithful devotee. At best, Trump could be qualified as a "new Christian" or even a "baby in the faith," as was said of him in 2016 by James Dobson, Christian psychologist and influential evangelical leader.[14]

Consequently, these evangelicals for Trump were neither upset nor scandalized by the words and actions of the former American president.

Evangelicals cited other biblical examples to defend favoring Trump despite his immoral conduct.[15] Franklin Graham, son of celebrated American evangelist Billy Graham,[16] vigorously defended himself prior to the election against those who called him out for his defense of such a morally corrupt candidate. He maintained that Trump was comparable to figures of the Old Testament, such as King David or the prophet Moses, and that greatness does not preclude imperfections.[17] It should be emphasized that Franklin Graham is a fervent supporter of the Christian right, a position in contrast to that of his father regarding political power after the debacle of the Nixon presidency in the Watergate affair. Graham's justifications regarding Trump include: The Bible does not excuse the adultery of King David with Bathsheba, Uriah's wife, nor the murder of her husband (2 Sam. 11–12); however, God forgave his sin (2 Sam. 12.13). Despite his faults, biblical authors presented David as "a man after (God's) own heart" (1 Sam. 13.13–14; 1 Kings 14.8; Acts 13.22). According to Graham, even the great prophet Moses disobeyed God and was punished (see Num. 20.7–12), but this did not prevent him from being a great liberator. Some critics, however, are surprised by the "ethical naiveté" of those who compared Trump to King David: according to Mark Galli, former editor-in-chief of an influential evangelical magazine, the difference between Trump and King David is that King David repented, while Donald Trump never did so![18]

For similar reasons, Rob McCoy, senior pastor of Godspeak Calvary Chapel and former mayor of Thousand Oaks, California, also compared Trump to the heroic figure Samson who, despite his immoral life, was the instrument of God for the destruction of his enemies (see Judg. 13–16). According to this reading, "Samson was willing to do what God's people weren't—confront the evil in their culture."[19] Regarding a different issue, that of the Iranian menace toward the Jewish people, former Secretary of State Mike Pompeo, an evangelical, also compared President Trump to the figure of Queen Esther: "President Trump right now has been sort of raised for such a time as this, just like Queen Esther, to help save the Jewish people from an Iranian menace."[20] In this case, it is not the immoral character of a biblical figure which serves as example, but rather their courage (Esth. 7). As with Esther, who defended the Jewish people against the murderous schemes of Haman, vizier of the Persian King Xerxes in the 5th century BCE (Esth. 3), Trump would also attack the Machiavellian plans of the Iranians—the Persians of biblical times—against the Jews.

This list would be incomplete without addressing the juxtaposition of Trump and Jesus. Indeed, before Trump's 2019 impeachment trial even began, some Republican senators established a parallel between the trial of Jesus before Pontius Pilate and that of the American president before

Congress. According to Georgia Republican senator Barry Loudermilk: "When Jesus was falsely accused of treason, Pontius Pilate gave Jesus the opportunity to face his accusers. During that sham trial, Pontius Pilate afforded more rights to Jesus than Democrats have afforded this president in this process."[21] Fred Keller, another Republican senator from Pennsylvania, mentioned Jesus' crucifixion, adding that he would pray for God to forgive the Democrats for the vote they were about to take against the president. In each of these cases, Trump's political mandate was confirmed by a typological and subjectivized reading of biblical characters and events.

Among the references mentioned above, the comparison with King Cyrus remains the most cited. It is not surprising that a few weeks before his death in October 2016, C. Peter Wagner, principal leader of the New Apostolic Reformation, endorsed Donald Trump as his favored candidate for the American presidency. Wagner said he wanted to vote for a "commander-in-chief" not a "bishop-in-chief!"[22] Lance Wallnau envisioned a similar scenario: Trump would be a secular reformer siding with evangelical Christians, thereby creating conditions favorable for bringing about a spiritual revival in the United States.

Heads Cyrus, Tails Trump

Comparisons were also made between Trump and Cyrus in the context of foreign policy. In 2018, Israeli Prime Minister Benjamin Netanyahu compared Trump to King Cyrus in relation to the relocation of the American embassy from Tel Aviv to Jerusalem. In 2017, Trump declared that Jerusalem was the capital of Israel, and later in 2019, he recognized Israel's sovereignty over the Golan Heights. But in 2018, Netanyahu had already made the comparison between Trump and the Persian king:

> I want to tell you that the Jewish people have a long memory, so we remember the proclamation of the great king, Cyrus the Great, the Persian king 2,500 years ago. He proclaimed that the Jewish exiles in Babylon could come back and rebuild our Temple in Jerusalem. We remember a hundred years ago, Lord Balfour, who issued the Balfour Proclamation that recognized the rights of the Jewish people in our ancestral homeland. We remember 70 years ago, President Harry S. Truman was the first leader to recognize the Jewish state. And we remember how a few weeks ago, President Donald J. Trump recognized Jerusalem as Israel's capital. Mr. President, this will be remembered by our people through the ages.[23]

Lance Wallnau was delighted by the American president's popularity in Israel and soon capitalized on it. In 2019, Wallnau undertook production of a coin with the image of Trump and Cyrus together on one side, and a quote taken from Isaiah 45.1[24] on the other. This initiative was not original; the education center Mikdash had already produced a coin with the image of the two leaders some months before.[25] Wallnau echoed their idea with the purpose of promoting Donald Trump's re-election. In the section on his website dedicated to the sale of products, Wallnau explains the significance of the coin. The *"Presidential Prayer Coin"* commemorates the "70th year" of the Cyrus–Trump announcement, wherein God would sovereignly appoint those serving to establish his Kingdom on earth. Wallnau continues with a Christian Zionist anecdote:

> On December 6th, 2017, while articles were being published the President shocked the world and declared that the United States would be moving its embassy from Tel Aviv to Jerusalem. This decision validates the right of Israel to exist as a nation-state with its historic capital in Jerusalem.
>
> Dispersed among nations until 1947, having survived the Nazi purge that took 6 million lives, the Jewish people miraculously regathered and formed as a struggling nation-state. As Israel celebrated its 70th anniversary (1947–2017) Donald Trump (this modern-day Cyrus) made the announcement that shook the spirit realm, just like Cyrus of old did in fulfilling a 70 year prophecy in his time, delivered by Jeremiah who foretold 70 years captivity for his people in Babylon. The captivity was ended by king Cyrus decree that the Jews to return back to Jerusalem.
>
> This bold U.S. announcement triggered shock waves that provoked a United Nations backlash. Suddenly, every nation was required to take a stand and vote either for or against the right of Israel to exist. A new era of history has begun where nations are entering "the valley of decision" and the issue involves Israel. Despite fierce opposition from America's allies: European and Arab world leaders alike, (including Britain, France, Germany, Saudi Arabia, Jordan, Egypt and even the Pope) said that President Trump was recklessly challenging a delicate status quo. The very U.N. that legitimized the existence of Israel in 1947 now voted to keep it from its final legitimization as a sovereign nation.[26]

Wallnau claimed that God had brought about a new Cyrus as a means of extending his mercy not only to the United States and for the good of his people, Israel, but also for the benefit of believers worldwide. In effect, Wallnau used his coin like a monetary exchange, operating as a sort of divine transaction between God and believers. To do this, he first had to convince Charismatics of the importance of Trump's re-election in November 2020. He called on them to pray for the president to be protected against the forces of the enemy (i.e., Satan and his minions), using the coin with the Trump-Cyrus relief like a "point of contact" with the president:

I know that if you could you would go to Washington D.C. yourself and encourage him, but right now I believe the Lord has given us two things we can do in the spirit realm that will impact this battle.

EVERY TIME you see this coin, TAKE IT IN YOUR HAND as a point of contact and pray. [...].

THIS IS ONE WAY WE CAN JOIN THE FIGHT IN THE SPIRIT. By praying for rulers, we are obeying what the Bible tells us to do and in this particular instance we are also breaking off of us the sliming effect we experience by being exposed to the daily barrage of toxicity, malice, deception and manipulation poured out through media, counterfeit investigators ... and the politicians [...].

WE GET STRONGER DOING THIS TOGETHER!

Wouldn't you be stronger just knowing that every time you take that coin in your hand and pray and decree that you are joined by 1000, 5000 or 10,000 other believers doing the same thing each day?[27]

Wallnau promoted his coin—which he sold for the modest price of $45—during an appearance on the *Jim Bakker Show*[28] in May 2019. He again stressed the idea that the coin constituted a "point of contact" which would allow millions of Christians to join in collective prayer as they beseeched God for protection, peace, and wisdom for Donald Trump and his family. Wallnau ended his plea with the claim that Christians were engaged in a battle for the future of America. They must now channel their optimism so the miracle that God had begun could continue.[29]

The idea that a physical object could serve as a "point of contact" is one shared by some Charismatics. Appeals to the Bible are made to justify this practice. Richard Roberts, son of the late American preacher Oral Roberts, explained that answers to prayer require the release of one's faith. The use of a physical object may prove helpful in communicating with God.

A point of contact is something you do. It's an action you take, in faith, as a deliberate, tangible moment when you can say you released your faith to God for what you need. It's like turning the key to start your car. When you do it, you expect something to happen. It helps you *focus your faith* on God and let go of any doubt. [...]

It's not how much faith you have, it's what you do with your faith that can make the difference.

You see, your faith has to be released before it can produce any results ... it has to come out of you and go up to God as an act of your believing.

A point of contact can be many different things: a prayer, anointing oil, a prayer cloth, Holy Communion, a faith-filled letter ... it's simply a method we can use to reach out to God.[30]

Roberts bases this idea in a literal and decontextualized interpretation of various biblical texts:

14[35] And when the men of that place recognized Jesus, they sent word to all the surrounding country. People brought all their sick to him[36] and begged him to let the sick just touch the edge of his cloak, and all who touched it were healed.

Matthew 14.35–36

5[12] The apostles performed many signs and wonders among the people …[15] As a result, people brought the sick into the streets and laid them on beds and mats so that at least **Peter's shadow might fall on some of them as he passed by.**

Acts 5.12 and 15

19[11] God did extraordinary miracles through Paul,[12] so that even **handkerchiefs and aprons that had touched him** were taken to the sick, and their illnesses were cured and the evil spirits left them.

Acts 19.11–12

The "point of contact" is a means of materializing faith, whether one is praying for healing, a financial miracle, divine protection, or something else. Note that these physical objects also create a lucrative market for Charismatic preachers. As derivative products, their value comes from the "anointing" they are believed to carry.[31] The peddling of small vials of olive oil is a common example:

In many Pentecostal and charismatic religious services, olive oil is believed to be a symbolic "point of contact" for anointing. A point of contact is an item used for transferring divine power to people … leaders use olive oil to coerce people into giving money. Since olive oil was believed to be a special substance for getting God's anointing, a prosperity preacher would look out into the crowd and make an offer for an anointed exchange. It was God's anointing being applied to your life for healing, money, conception of children, job promotions, and more in exchange for a monetary offering that would be prayed over and anointed with the oil. It was a divine transaction that appealed to the deepest human needs.[32]

For Wallnau, the Trump-Cyrus coin played the same role: in exchange for a monetary gift of $45, it became a rallying point for millions of Christians. When these Christians come together in prayer, they believe it will help them achieve their vision of establishing Christian dominion in the United States and around the world. They see it as a way to release their faith and fulfill their needs through a divine transaction.

Conquering the "Seven Mountains" of Culture

The idea of Donald Trump as a new Cyrus is an integral part of a particular theology of political power. Trump's election was instrumental in furthering the interests of the Charismatics who seek to shape society according to their values. For Wallnau, President Trump's rise to power would intensify and reform Christian activity in the United States. It would result in aligning the country's laws and institutions with biblical principles.[33] According to Wallnau, the faithful must reclaim the country's institutional "high places" (i.e., the places of power). To do so, they must occupy positions of influence in the secular culture,[34] which Wallnau believes, as we will shortly see, to be under demonic influence. Since the early 2000s, he has worked at formulating a strategy of societal transformation which he calls the "Seven Mountain Mandate."[35] The objective is to influence the spheres of religion, education, business, government, arts and entertainment, media, and the family.[36] The culmination of this vision is nothing less than the establishment of God's Kingdom on earth, conforming to a literal interpretation of the Our Father prayer: "your kingdom come, your will be done, on earth as it is in heaven" (Matt. 6.10).

How are the "Seven Mountains" defined and what must occur within each of these spheres of cultural influence to bring about societal transformation? To occupy the "mountain of religion" the Church must actively engage in proclaiming the Gospel message and make disciples of all the nations, working to establish and expand God's Kingdom worldwide. To influence the "mountain of education" requires reintroducing biblical values and truth into a failed education system to counter the secular indoctrination of students. To ascend the "business mountain" entails church leaders training business owners to assure integrity and honest leadership in the labor and stock markets, a commitment accompanied by promises of economic prosperity, because God wishes to enrich his people in ways that will permit financing the work of expanding his earthly Kingdom. It is necessary to conquer the "mountain of government (politics)" by supporting leaders with integrity who would have a positive influence on government policies, in particular, the preservation of the Christian heritage on which evangelicals assert the United States was founded. The influence on today's youth coming from the "mountain of arts and entertainment" (music, film, television, sports, social media, etc.) must come from people with integrity who use their talents in service to God's Kingdom. The transformation of the "mountain of the media" (radio, news stations, newspapers, news and opinion websites, blogs, etc.) will occur through Christians working to eradicate "fake news" and taking control of the mainstream media—not just the religious media—to broadcast the news honestly. Finally, a revolution is hoped for on the "mountain of the family," seen as the cornerstone of functional societies. The goal here is to promote the return to a patriarchal model in heterosexual relationships and to what is understood as the traditional family structure (hence opposing abortion, same-sex families and marriages, and other LGBTQ+ rights).

The "Seven Mountain Mandate" is profoundly shaped by a political theology of power known as "dominionism," according to which Christians are called by God to rule (i.e., exercise authority) over all aspects of society by controlling political and cultural institutions—regardless of the point of view, means, or theological perspective.[37] Fundamentally, the idea is that Christians are called to exercise dominion in the world. This view is based on a unique understanding of Genesis 1.26–28, as translated in the King James Version:[38]

1[26] And God said, Let us make man in our image, after our likeness: and let them have *dominion* over the fish of the sea, and over the fowl of the air, and over the cattle, and over all the earth, and over every creeping thing that creepeth upon the earth.[27] So God created man in his own image, in the image of God created he him; male and female created he them.[28] And God blessed them, and God said unto them, Be fruitful, and multiply, and replenish the earth, and *subdue* it: and have *dominion* over the fish of the sea, and over the fowl of the air, and over every living thing that moveth upon the earth."

In the United States, this theology of political power is primarily found among the Christian right. Its political aims are centered around opposing LGBTQ+ rights and sex education, advocating anti-abortion activism, promoting prayer and teaching of creationism or intelligent design in public schools, and protecting their religious freedom.[39]

The Christian right in the United States includes (1) Christian conservatives, (2) Christian nationalists, and (3) Christian theocrats.[40] Christian conservatives do not necessarily have a "dominionist" view. Their primary objective is to preserve their own conservative values in the society, without the implementation of a Christian hegemony. Christian nationalists believe the United States was founded as a Christian nation and must return to its roots. For nationalists, Christianity must have primacy over other religions, and religious freedom is seen first and foremost as a right specific to Christians. Christian theocrats, on the other hand, claim that divine law—such as the Ten Commandments—should be the foundation of American political and social order. Some "dominionist" Christians strive to enact their reforms not only in the United States, but also globally. For them, Jesus calls his own to "make disciples of all the nations," teaching them to keep his commandments, because all power is given to him over heaven and earth (Matt. 28.18–20). But how can they accomplish such a task?

Rebuilding a Christian Society

"Dominionism," as commonly understood today, is mainly associated with "Christian reconstructionism," a movement that emerged in the 1960s and 1970s. The movement's founder, Rousas J. Rushdoony (1916–2001),[41] was a Presbyterian minister known for his numerous publications.[42] He obtained a bachelor's degree in English Studies and a master's in Education from the University of California at Berkeley in 1938.[43] He also completed a bachelor's in Pastoral Studies at the Pacific School of Religion in Berkeley in 1944 and was later ordained in the Presbyterian Church USA (PCUSA). He was awarded two honorary doctorates: one by Brainerd Theological Seminary in 1975, and the other by Grove City College in 1978. Rushdoony completed a doctorate in Education at Valley Christian University in 1980 and published *The Philosophy of the Christian Curriculum* the following year.[44] From 1944 to 1953, Rushdoony held his first pastorate as leader of a missionary church in the small town of Owyhee, Nevada, on the Duck Valley Indian Reservation.[45] In 1953, Rushdoony became pastor in a PCUSA parish in Santa Cruz, California. Five years later, disillusioned with the PCUSA, he left the denomination to join the Orthodox Presbyterian Church. Supported by a group who shared his grievances, he opened a small church in Santa Cruz. Rushdoony left the ministry in 1962, taking a research position at the Center for American Studies the following year. The Center believed Rushdoony's doctrinal views to be too sectarian, however, and he was subsequently asked to leave. Finally, in 1965, Rushdoony founded The Chalcedon Foundation,[46] an organization dedicated to the teaching, research, publication, and promotion of Christian reconstructionism.

What are the tenets of this political theology? Reconstructionist theology[47] derives its contemporary expression from the teachings of Augustine,[48] Calvin,[49] and neo-Calvinist theologians Abraham Kuyper[50] and Cornelius Van Til.[51] Influenced by Calvinism,[52] Christian reconstructionism places great emphasis on the sovereignty of God. Like many evangelicals, Rushdoony held that each domain or sphere of life must be aligned with the Bible's teachings, the sole source of truth and authority for every believer. The movement also teaches theonomy (biblical law)[53] and seeks to "reconstruct" American society on Christian principles—hence the name "Christian reconstructionism."

Putting divine law into practice in the realms of family, church, and civil government must be done progressively. Rushdoony had a two-pronged approach to social transformation. In the short term, he believed in participating in electoral politics to influence elected officials. However, he also had a long-term strategy that involved identifying and supporting competent leaders who shared his vision of establishing God's Kingdom. Rushdoony stressed this latter course and believed that parent-led Christian education, specifically through homeschooling, was the best means to accomplish this goal. Children raised in a traditional "Judeo-Christian" home were then expected to become agents of transformation.

Rushdoony's sociopolitical vision is laid out in *The Institutes of Biblical Law*.[54] In his *magnum opus*, Rushdoony vigorously defended the idea of a society ruled by biblical laws, where the power of the state is limited. Rushdoony envisioned a society where citizens would denounce criminals who would be forced to compensate their victims; where those who commit the worst crimes would be executed, making prisons superfluous in the long run; and where the environment would be managed according to "biblical principles" (quite far, according to this interpretation, from any ecological concern).

Transformation Apostles

Although many American Christians were skeptical of the strictest parts of the reconstructionist model, there has been increasing interest in the idea of social transformation.[55] In 1975, three years after the publication of Rushdoony's work, two influential evangelical leaders, Bill Bright, founder of Campus Crusade for Christ,[56] and Loren Cunningham, founder of Youth With A Mission,[57] both independently claimed to have received divine revelations concerning the "Seven Mountains" of culture.[58] However, according to Joel McDurmon,[59] the circumstances surrounding these self-proclaimed revelations are altogether suspect:

> This book (*The Institutes of Biblical Law*) was in development for five long years while Rushdoony preached through the Mosaic law, applying it to every area of life. Bright and Cunningham were in the same area of California at the time. [...] the alleged revelation to these men seems to have taken key notes from Rushdoony's earlier publication.[60]

Although the origins of these revelations are unclear, it's important to note that the social transformation concept adopted by Charismatic Christians is significantly different from the neo-Calvinist perspective. This has affected Christian reconstructionism, where the focus is on God's sovereignty. Christian reconstructionists mostly strive for a slow and progressive "bottom up" transformation of society, a more passive approach which sees God establishing his Kingdom in his own time, according to his sovereign plan. The "Seven Mountains" approach completely upends this vision. Charismatic "dominionists" encourage believers to become actively involved in God's work.[61] It is no longer a question, as was the case with Rushdoony, of waiting for God's sovereign action.[62] Hence the "Seven Mountain Mandate" is understood as a "top-down" takeover, leaning toward a more aggressive form of dominionism, one seemingly less passive than that of Christian reconstructionism.

This dominionist variant finds its full expression in the New Apostolic Reformation's political theology. In fact, in 2008, C. Peter Wagner wrote a very influential book: *Dominion! How Kingdom Action Can Change the World*. Wagner recognized his debt to Calvinist thinkers such as Kuyper and Rushdoony in the development of his view of dominion.[63] In a letter to the financial supporters of his Global Harvest Ministries organization dated May 31, 2007, (prior to publication of *Dominion!*) Wagner had already explained the dominionist character of his ministry:

> Our theological bedrock is what has been known as Dominion Theology. This means that our divine mandate is to do whatever is necessary, by the power of the Holy Spirit, to retake the dominion of God's creation which Adam forfeited to Satan in the Garden of Eden. It is nothing less than seeing God's kingdom coming and His will being done here on earth as it is in heaven. [...] We want to see whole cities and regions and states and nations transformed to support the values of the kingdom of God. This will happen only as kingdom-focused saints become the head and not the tail ...[64]

This dominion model proceeds "from the top down," as suggested by the reference to becoming "the head and not the tail."[65] As the main leader of the New Apostolic Reformation,[66] Wagner expressed his approval of Lance Wallnau's work. The latter claimed to have been introduced to "Seven Mountains" by Loren Cunningham in 2000 and admited to never having heard of this concept before.[67] Since then, Wallnau has become one of the biggest promoters of the "Seven Mountain Mandate." In 2007, Wagner was already presenting him as a rising star of the Apostolic networks:[68]

> The major catalyst whom God has brought into the picture to help renew our minds in terms of our philosophy of mission is Lance Wallnau, founder of Lance Learning Group currently based in Rhode Island. Lance, in a former season, planted churches and formed an apostolic network which he has now turned over to other leadership. He is a member of ICA [International Coalition of Apostles], and he currently travels widely as a conference speaker and as a consultant to business and government leaders. Through the years we have formed a close relationship, he has been a speaker at several of our conferences ...
> Lance's trademark teaching relates to what he calls the seven "mind molders" or the "seven mountains." These have now become a permanent fixture in my personal teaching on taking dominion, and I have referenced

Wallnau in *The Church in the Workplace* as well as in my forthcoming book *Dominion!* In my view it is not possible to get an operational handle on how to initiate corporate action toward social transformation without taking into account the seven mountains or what I like to call "molders of culture." The seven [mountains] are religion, family, business, arts & entertainment, government, education, and media.[69]

Thus, the New Apostolic Reformation, under the aegis of chief Apostle C. Peter Wagner, became involved in the "Seven Mountain Mandate." In this light, Wagner's support for Donald Trump's presidential ambitions becomes understandable. In Trump, he saw characteristics of a modern-day Cyrus and was convinced of the billionaire's influence on the "business mountain." For Wagner, if spirituality is necessary to influence the "religion mountain," a corollary should apply for society's other high (non-religious) places. Wagner claimed that Trump, thanks to his fortune, could have access to the summits of the mountains of business, arts and entertainment, and the media.[70] He argued that the most successful people are the most influential, with Trump's role as an influencer clear to all around him. Moreover, if Donald Trump is chosen by God *à la* Cyrus, it is not surprising that Charismatics made the choice to elect a leader having power in certain cultural spheres. This power and influence coincide with being "the head and not the tail" (Deut. 28.13).

Trump's role as the new Cyrus is directly linked to the Charismatic dominion strategy. It was Wallnau who had popularized the idea of Trump as a modern-day Cyrus, and he is the dominant figure associated with the "Seven Mountains" of culture. Trump-Cyrus would be the instrument of divine chaos chosen to break the status quo and lead American society in its final days, fulfilling God's will for the nation. This was the reason Wallnau published *God's Chaos Candidate: Donald J. Trump and the American Unraveling*, a book whose central thesis is that "Trump was the new element introduced [by God] in history that produced immediate chaos all over the world," this divine upheaval opening believers to new possibilities, on both individual and societal levels.[71]

Charlie Kirk, founder and president of Turning Point USA, a national conservative student movement,[72] voiced a comparable view. During a meeting of the Conservative Political Action Conference in 2020, he stated: "Finally, we have a president that understands the seven mountains of cultural influence!"[73] Rob McCoy took a similar stance, explaining Trump's influence on the cultural mountains during a February 2020 meeting:

There's seven mountains of cultural influence: arts and entertainment, media, business, politics, religion, education, and family. And of those seven mountains of cultural influence there's a currency in each one of them. In politics, it's winning elections, in media, in arts and entertainment it's selling movie tickets, etc. So, let's look at moving that culture, and let's look at the current president. Arts and entertainment: he had the number one television show in America; media: he's mastered the Twitter world; politics: he took out seventeen Republican candidates and the most heavily funded Democrat candidate in the history of the nation; business: the Trump brand is world renowned. We can just go through the whole thing. This is a man who's equipped. And if you don't like him, fine—but you know why God picked him? Because there were no Christians available. Now some of the candidates running were Christians, but were they equipped in every mountain of cultural influence?[74]

The "Seven Mountains" strategy is not a method whereby Christians engage in individual evangelization, seeking to convert their loved ones one at a time. New Apostolic Reformation teaching holds that Jesus commands his followers to "make disciples of all nations" (*cf.* Matt. 28.18–20). It is a call to reform populations, i.e., political communities. This mandate targets cultural influence and social transformation to bring all nations into alignment with the values of the Kingdom of God.[75] Lance Wallnau explains how believers can strategically penetrate the "matrix of this world" to invade and influence each cultural system:

The business of shifting culture or transforming nations does not require a majority of conversions. We make a mistake when we focus on winning a harvest in order [to] shape a culture. Together, Protestants and Catholics make up a 70 percent majority of the U.S. population, and such already have a majority consensus on key matters affecting marriage and abortion. Yet they are still incapable of being more than a firewall to the minority, who are advancing a same-sex ideology. If we do not need more conversions to shift a culture, what do we need? We need more disciples in the right places, the high places. Minorities of people can shape the agenda, if properly aligned and deployed. [...] The Church lacks cultural power because it focuses on changing the world from within the Church mountain rather than releasing the Church into the marketplace ... The goal is to be the Church that raises up disciples who go into all the world. [...] The world is a matrix of overlapping systems or spheres of influence. We are called to go into the entire matrix and invade every system with an influence that liberates that system's fullest potential ... Each sphere has a unique structure, culture, and [...] a worldview of its own. The battle in each sphere is over the ideas that dominate that sphere and between the individuals who have the most power to advance those ideas ... The Church must be represented in each sphere if the power of darkness is [to] be broken.[76]

This cultural imperative could not be accomplished without the commitment of the faithful. But how does one incite and train disciples for the task of making "a breakthrough around the world" and going through "the whole matrix" with the goal to "invade and influence each system"? It is here that Wagner's vision of church reform comes in, along with his theology of apostolic governance.

Notes

1 See video extract: https://www.youtube.com/watch?v=He7y6XTU52k/ (accessed 22 May 2023).
2 See Wallnau's website: https://lancewallnau.com/about/ (accessed 22 May 2023).
3 This institution, founded in 1963 by American preacher Oral Roberts, is a private charismatic evangelical university located in Tulsa, Oklahoma. ORU enrolls around 4000 students.
4 Evangelicals refer to certain biblical texts when speaking of the "new birth" (see John 1.12–13; 3.3, and 2 Cor. 5.17).
5 Evangelicals also justify this practice of baptism from the Acts of the Apostles (see 2.37–41; 8.5–13, 36–38; 9.10–12, etc.).
6 The significance of this experience is explained in the introduction.
7 The academic value of such an institution is questionable. See the commentary of Warren Throckmorton concerning this institution and Wallnau's diploma: https://www.wthrockmorton.com/2017/01/02/world-phoenix-university-theology/ (accessed 22 May 2023).
8 Part of Wallnau's history is available here: https://fgbt.org/Testimonies/lance-wallnau-story.html/ (accessed 28 February 2020).
9 Wallnau: "Donald Trump is a wrecking ball to the spirit of political correctness." See J. S. Gordon, "Does the 'Cyrus prophecy' help explain evangelical support for Donald Trump?" *The Guardian*, 23 March 2017: https://www.theguardian.com/commentisfree/2017/mar/23/cyrus-prophecy-evangelical-support-donald-trump/ (accessed 22 May 2023).
10 Unless indicated otherwise, biblical quotes are taken from the New International Version (*NIV*).
11 In Hebrew, the term *mashiah* means "anoint" and designates a person chosen by God, ordained with a divine mission.
12 See the BBC video: "President Trump: 'I am the chosen one'" https://www.bbc.com/news/av/world-us-canada-49429661/president-trump-i-am-the-chosen-one/ (accessed 22 May 2023).
13 See other biblical references to King Cyrus and the liberation of the Jewish people in 2 Chron. 36.22–23, and Ezra 1.1–11.
14 https://www.christianitytoday.com/news/2016/august/james-dobson-explains-why-donald-trump-baby-christian.html/ (accessed 22 May 2023).
15 Peter Montgomery lists the reasons evangelicals give for claiming that Trump is "God's Guy": https://www.rightwingwatch.org/post/gods-guy-25-religious-right-justifications-for-supporting-donald-trump/ (accessed 22 May 2023).
16 The Grahams, both father and son, are not part of the Charismatic branch of American evangelism but they are part of neo-evangelicalism.
17 https://www.christianpost.com/news/franklin-graham-to-900-evangelical-leaders-donald-trump-is-better-option-than-hillary-clinton-165487/#i8c5q8hkKb561HM4.99/ (accessed 22 May 2023).

18 https://www.nytimes.com/2020/01/02/us/christianity-today-mark-galli-evangelicals.html/ (accessed 22 May 2023).
19 https://www.rightwingwatch.org/post/charlie-kirk-teams-up-with-dominionists-and-christian-nationalists-to-wage-spiritual-war/ (accessed 22 May 2023).
20 https://slate.com/news-and-politics/2019/06/trump-evangelical-foreign-policy-pence-pompeo.html/ (accessed 22 May 2023).
21 https://www.washingtonpost.com/politics/2019/12/18/trumps-impeachment-is-like-jesuss-crucifixion-salem-witch-trials-pearl-harbor-all-rolled-into-one/ (accessed 22 May 2023).
22 C. Peter Wagner, "I Like Donald Trump," *Charisma News*, 6 October 2016: https://www.charismanews.com/politics/opinion/57707-c-peter-wagner-i-like-donald-trump/ (accessed 22 May 2023).
23 https://www.timesofisrael.com/who-is-king-cyrus-and-why-is-netanyahu-comparing-him-to-trump/ (accessed 22 May 2023).
24 Wallnau produced a video presenting the coin: https://vimeo.com/275716614/ (accessed 22 May 2023).
25 https://abcnews.go.com/International/israeli-group-sells-special-edition-trump-coin/story?id=55096698/ (accessed 22 May 2023).
26 https://lance-learning.myshopify.com/products/cyrus-trump-proclamation-prayer-coin/ (accessed 22 May 2023).
27 *Ibid.*
28 The *Jim Bakker Show* is a daily charismatic program focused on biblical "end times" prophecies and Christ's second coming. Bakker and his guests also regularly sell survivalist food and other products. Jim Bakker is an American televangelist and businessman. In 1992, he was sentenced to eight years in prison for fraud, but he returned to television in 2003 with the *Jim Bakker Show*, which he hosts with his second wife, Lori Beth Graham.
29 https://twitter.com/rightwingwatch/status/1128366601445810177?lang=en/ (accessed 22 May 2023).
30 https://oralroberts.com/point-of-contact/ (accessed 22 May 2023).
31 In Charismatic communities, "anointing" represents the spiritual power God grants believers to assure the effectiveness of their ministry.
32 Hinn (2019, p. 80).
33 Wallnau makes plain that Trump is not the only modern-day "Cyrus": "The 'Cyrus' word is not a term for Donald Trump exclusively. It is a term that describes a type of leader raised up by God for the benefit of the people of God and the protection of their sovereign nations whose borders, culture, identity, and uniqueness are under siege. These aspects that make up 'the glory of nations' are in danger of being lost to a vigorous end time effort ...": https://lancewallnau.com/the-era-of-cyrus-rulers/#more-22331/ (accessed 22 May 2023).
34 "Lance Wallnau: Why Trump Is 'God's Chaos Candidate' and 'Wrecking Ball'," *CBN News*, 21 March 2017: https://www1.cbn.com/cbnnews/us/2017/march/lance-wallnau-weighs-in-on-gods-chaos-candidate-now-americas-president/ (accessed 22 May 2023).
35 Lance Wallnau addresses the "7 Mountain Mandate"; see Wallnau (2010). For an in-depth analysis of the "Seven Mountains" of culture, see Gonzalez (2014, pp. 265–297).
36 As mentioned in the introduction, Wallnau now believes that the mountains of "arts and entertainment" has merged with that of "media" to make room for another mountain, that of "science and technology."
37 According to the definition of Political Research Associates scholar Frederick Clarkson: "Dominionism Rising: A Theocratic Movement Hiding in Plain Sight," *The Public Eye* (Summer 2016), pp. 12–20.

38 Emphases mine.
39 See André Gagné, « La droite chrétienne: « changer les mentalités » pour mieux transformer la société », *La Conversation Canada*, 23 July 2019: https:// theconversation.com/la-droite-chretienne-changer-les-mentalites-pour-mieux-transformer-la-societe-120563/ (accessed 22 May 2023).
40 The following categories were suggested by Chip Berlet, see http://www. talk2action.org/story/2005/12/5/10810/4239 (accessed 22 May 2023).
41 See McVicar (2015) concerning Rushdoony's life, work, and theological thought. See also Ingersoll (2015).
42 For a complete list of Rushdoony's publications, see https://www.scribd.com/ document/372092259/Rushdoony-Bibliography/ (accessed 22 May 2023).
43 The salient facts on Rushdoony's life are provided in a short biographical sketch on the Chalcedon Foundation site: https://chalcedon.edu/about/who-was-r-j-rushdoony/ (accessed 22 May 2023).
44 More information on Rushdoony's education is available at https://chalcedon. edu/magazine/rousas-john-rushdoony-a-brief-history-part-ii-you-are-going-to-be-a-writer/ (accessed 22 May 2023).
45 For more details on Rushdoony's pastoral years, see https://chalcedon.edu/ magazine/rousas-john-rushdoony-a-brief-history-part-iv-the-painful-years/ (accessed 22 May 2023).
46 See https://chalcedon.edu/ (accessed 22 May 2023).
47 For more, see Ingersoll (2015, pp. 14–16).
48 Augustine is one of the Fathers of the Latin (or Western) Church; he lived from 345 to 430 CE.
49 John Calvin (1509–1564) was a theologian, pastor, and important reformer during the Protestant Reformation of the 16th century.
50 Abraham Kuyper (1837–1920) was a theologian, journalist, and Dutch statesman. He led and brought to power an Orthodox Calvinist group called the Antirevolutionary Party and was prime minister of the Netherlands from 1901 to 1905.
51 Born in the Netherlands, Cornelius Van Til (1895–1987) was a Christian philosopher, a Reformed theologian, and a presuppositional apologist.
52 Calvinism, as a theological system, holds that all domains of life (social, political, ecclesial, and personal) must be conducted according to the sovereign will of God. One can sum up Calvinist (conservative) theology according to the following five principles: total depravity, unconditional election, limited atonement, irresistible grace, and perseverance of the saints.
53 "The law in force in any government (civil or otherwise) must be fully and exclusively taken from Holy Scriptures, directly or indirectly. Theonomy therefore advocates the reformation of spirituality, culture, economy, and law to align them with God's law as revealed in the Bible. Therefore, theonomy is incompatible with sociopolitical polytheism (commonly called multiculturalism or religious pluralism)." See http:// sentinellenehemie.free.fr/Theonomie_v4.0_180717.pdf (accessed 7 March 2020).
54 Rushdoony (1973); note that the title references John Calvin's tome, *Institutes of the Christian Religion*.
55 For an excellent synthesis of Rushdoony's influence on Francis Schaeffer's thinking see Gonzalez (2014, pp. 293–296).
56 In evangelical circles, Bright is best known for his "four spiritual laws," a pamphlet inspired by marketing techniques aiming to facilitate evangelical proselytizing: (1) God loves you and offers a wonderful plan for your life; (2) Man is sinful and separated from God; (3) Jesus Christ is the only means for God to save mankind from its sin; (4) We must individually receive Jesus Christ as Savior and Lord. See Turner (2008) for more information on Bright and his organization.

57 For more details on Cunningham and the Youth With a Mission organization, see Fer (2010).

58 Loren Cunningham recounts this miraculous story in 2007: https://youtu.be/iOrLz_RdOjQ/ (accessed 22 May 2023).

59 Joel McDurmon was president of The American Vision (https://americanvision.org/), an organization associated with "Christian reconstructionism" from 2015 to 2019. Financial concerns seem to have been the motive for his retirement from the organization in March 2019.

60 Joel McDurmon, "Biblical Dominion or Seven Mountain Dominion?," 1 November 2019: https://www.lambsreign.com/blog/biblical-dominion-or-seven-mountains-dominion/ (accessed 22 May 2023).

61 This type of activism is often linked to a theology known as "Arminian" which stresses the idea of human free will in the work of salvation while downplaying the Calvinist doctrine of predestination. Believers collaborate with God in the work of conversion.

62 Rushdoony's approach is "monergistic," i.e., the idea that salvation is an act of God alone, a perspective consistent with Calvinism.

63 Wagner (2008, pp. 59–60).

64 http://www.fulfilledprophecy.com/discussion/viewtopic.php?f=9&t=26653/ (accessed 24 February 2020).

65 This expression comes from Deuteronomy 28.13: "The Lord will make you the head, not the tail. If you pay attention to the commands of the Lord your God that I give you this day and carefully follow them, you will always be at the top, never at the bottom." See also Gonzalez (2014, pp. 284–287) concerning the usage of this expression by some neo-Charismatics.

66 For more information on the different beliefs and practices associated with the New Apostolic Reformation movement, see https://adioma.com/@ChristianRight Xposed/infographic/beliefs-and-practices-of-the-nar/ (accessed 22 May 2023).

67 Wallnau (2010, pp. 177–178); see also: https://youtu.be/qQbGnJd9poc/ (accessed 22 May 2023).

68 The next chapter will be dedicated to the concept and function of apostolic networks.

69 http://www.fulfilledprophecy.com/discussion/viewtopic.php?f=9&t=26653/ (accessed 24 February 2020).

70 C. Peter Wagner, "I Like Donald Trump," *Charisma News*, 6 October 2016: https://www.charismanews.com/politics/opinion/57707-c-peter-wagner-i-like-donald-trump/ (accessed 22 May 2023).

71 See Wallnau's video, *God's End Time Endgame*: https://www.youtube.com/watch?v=iEU95ZSGm_8/ (accessed 2 March 2020).

72 This movement is present on more than 2000 high school and college campuses across America.

73 https://www.youtube.com/watch?v=c-WiaPPxIHc/ (accessed 22 May 2023).

74 https://www.youtube.com/watch?v=NC7X2YaR9jU/ (accessed 22 May 2023).

75 Wagner (2008, pp. 72–73).

76 Wallnau (2010, pp. 186–187).

2

APOSTLES

Religious and Political Entrepreneurs

According to C. Peter Wagner, the New Apostolic Reformation gave rise to the most important transformation of Protestantism since the 16th-century reformation![1] Wagner believed that the United States entered in 2001 into what he called a second apostolic age.[2] The New Apostolic Reformation is not a denomination per se, but more akin to a post-denominational movement. A "denomination" is a subgroup within Protestantism sharing a common name, identity, and similar traditions. Denominations are generally democratic and operate under identical administrative and governmental structures. Conversely, this post-denominational movement resists the institutional and democratic type of organization found in most denominations, to the effect of deregulating the traditional church government model. The churches which share the New Apostolic Reformation paradigm have similar beliefs and practices, certainly, but their approach is not institutional; they are linked through interpersonal networks. Among the founding pastors leading these churches, rare are those who have formal theological training. Most claim to have received a "call from God" ordaining them to establish their church. Wagner claims to find theological justification for his New Apostolic Reformation style of governance in an often-quoted text of the New Testament:

4[11] So Christ himself gave the apostles, the prophets, the evangelists, the pastors and teachers,[12] to equip his people for works of service, so that the body of Christ may be built up[13] until we all reach unity in the faith and in the knowledge of the Son of God and become mature, attaining to the whole measure of the fullness of Christ.

Ephesians 4.11–13

DOI: 10.4324/9781003358718-3

According to Wagner, the existence of modern-day apostles and prophets is justified by the fact that their purpose is to "equip" God's people for "the works of service so that the body of Christ may be built up" until the Church* (understood here in its universal, invisible sense) attains full maturity. But what, then are "apostles" and "prophets" according to the New Apostolic Reformation?

An apostle is an ambassador (of the church) who exercises a representative form of government on God's behalf.[3] As a Christian leader, an apostle is gifted, educated, and granted authority by God, and is responsible for adequately managing the Church in a clearly delineated ministerial capacity. Apostles are sensitive to how the Holy Spirit leads the Church for the advancement of God's Kingdom on earth.[4] In exercising their leadership, apostles also gain the support of other leaders to carry out their mission.[5] This support, or "apostolic attraction," in turn unleashes the principle of "apostolic alignment," which is an appeal for other responsible Christians to recognize the authority of the apostle and place themselves under his "cover"—a term implying protection and accountability.[6] This type of "alignment" is mainly done by apostles having a "vertical function" [*Vertical Apostles*]. According to Wagner, most apostles exercise a vertical role. They either oversee church networks, ministries, or individuals to which they provide "spiritual cover."[7]

Prophets, on the other hand, are individuals recognized as recipients of a particular inspiration of the Holy Spirit, allowing them to receive supernatural revelation from God. According to the New Apostolic Reformation model of church governance, prophets collaborate with apostles, communicating the content of their revelations, to ensure the sound management of churches for the expansion God's Kingdom.[8]

Wagner claims that the Church* is far from having realized a state of perfection—hence the need to establish contemporary apostolic and prophetic ministries[9] as a foundation for building the Church*.[10] For many New Apostolic Reformation leaders, modern-day apostles have a preeminent role in the Church, according to their understanding of a text from the Apostle Paul:

12[28] And God has placed in the church *first of all apostles*, second prophets, third teachers, then miracles, then gifts of healing, of helping, of guidance, and of different kinds of tongues.

1 Corinthians 12.28

Whatever the relationship between apostles and prophets, the New Apostolic Reformation church model appeals to various New Testament texts, while omitting other important passages. Many people often overlook the historical context of the first Christian communities. Supporters of the New Apostolic Reformation model interpret Scripture in a way which minimizes the reception of the Bible and lessons from church history. Their view is contrary to that of traditional churches which operate according to a democratic model of church governance.

Their reference to Ephesians 4 not only accounts for the role they assign to contemporary apostles and prophets but also for that of Christians who, according to this reading, must be trained for "works of service." From a Charismatic perspective, this theological concept corresponds to Christ's commission entrusted to believers to build up the Church* by means of spiritual gifts granted by the Holy Spirit, for the advancement of God's Kingdom.[11] It is here that the "Seven Mountains" strategy finds its purpose. When Wallnau urges the Church* to "go into the entire matrix and invade every system with an influence that liberates that system's fullest potential,"[12] he is referring to the "works of service" (i.e., "the ministry") which believers must carry out in their own spheres of influence. Every believer must climb and conquer his "mountain"—his place of activity and influence—with the goal of bringing about the hoped-for cultural transformation. Believers become what Wagner calls "apostles at work" or "the Church* at work."[13] Kingdom "conquest" is therefore extended to one's professional life.

In the remainder of this chapter, we examine two types of apostolic transitions. First, we will see how apostles transform local churches into "apostolic centers." We will then examine how these centers, once established, serve to develop "apostolic networks." The objective of this secondary transformational phase is to push Christians outside the walls of the church, aligning them with religious and political entrepreneurs within other existing apostolic networks.

From Local Church to Apostolic Center

Training "apostles at work" is carried out through "apostolic centers." These spaces focus on developing and activating Christians to participate in the mission of transforming society. In this section, one example will be provided of this type of transition from church to apostolic center involving a small francophone congregation in Québec. This example will illustrate the extent to which the New Apostolic Reformation is a transnational movement, the impact of which extends beyond the United States or indeed the English-speaking world.

Inspired by Wagner's vision, Apostle Alain Caron of the apostolic center Le Chemin [*The Way*], located in Gatineau, Québec, is the founder of the apostolic network HODOS.[14] Le Chemin was founded in 1975 by Jean-Claude Joyal and his wife Valerie as l'Église du Chemin du Calvaire [*Church of the Way of Calvary*]. Following a conversion experience, Alain Caron joined the community in 1987. In the late 1990s, Pastor Joyal turned the church leadership over to Caron, who has taken responsibility for it since then.

As we will see, this church gradually shifted toward an "apostolic" model in 2010–2011. Today, Le Chemin's apostolic center is a multi-ethnic congregation with a few hundred members, mainly from the Gatineau region. The apostolic team comprises about 25 people, dispatched to three different locations. The meetings which take place in the Gatineau and East-Gatineau areas are conducted in French and English, Canada's two official languages. Meetings held in Maniwaki, a town in the province of Québec, some 135 km (84 miles) north of Gatineau, are conducted in French.

Caron is one of the first authors to write a book explaining how to transform a church into an apostolic center.[15] In a similar vein, on the HODOS network website, he recounts the two-year process by which his church became an apostolic center and describes his vision.[16]

If the New Apostolic Reformation is the latest and most advanced phase of the global development plan, what are the key steps that will lead us from new wineskins to new wine?[17]

Convinced that the New Apostolic Reformation represents the last phase of God's worldwide plan for the Church, Caron asked himself how to bring about this metamorphosis, which he called passing "from new wineskins to new wine." The symbolism of "new wineskins" and "new wine" comes from a parable in which Jesus describes the novelty of his teaching: "And no one pours new wine into old wineskins. Otherwise, the new wine will burst the skins; the wine will run out and the wineskins will be ruined. No, new wine must be poured into new wineskins" (Luke 5.37–38).

By Caron's rationale, the "wineskin" represents the way a church or denomination operates. Generally, churches function according to a collaborative leadership model, with leaders accountable to the congregation in matters concerning financial management and decision-making.[18] According to Caron, this governance model, formerly that of his church, corresponds to an "old wineskin": the church is placed in charge of a team of faithful believers (the "board of elders") which is elected somewhat democratically—even though this model remains oligarchic and patriarchal as women rarely ascend to these positions. The New Testament also designates "elders" as pastoral leaders with the responsibility of overseeing the spiritual well-being of their Christian communities (see Acts 14.23; 20.17; 1 Tim. 3.1–7; Tit. 1.5–9; 1 Pet. 5.1–2.4; Jas. 5.14). In most traditional evangelical churches, the elders are elected by the congregation. Prospective candidates for these positions are chosen for their "integrity" and according to biblical criteria. The church pastor is also elected by the congregation, with the recommendation of the board of elders, and is part of the leadership team. The pastor and the elders are then beholden to the congregation, which must ensure that the leaders do not abuse their authority (far from an easy task). From the perspective of the New Apostolic Reformation, however, the traditional ecclesial structure is seen as a "sacred cow" which must be slain:[19] the pastor's traditional role as principal leader of a Christian community must disappear in favor of an apostolic model.

Caron explains that the idea of the apostolic center is "flexible and mobile"[20]—here, the vocabulary is typically managerial in nature.[21] The Church must adapt to the reality of a competing "religious market": different chapels and denominations are vying to attract "followers," and those who offer the best "product" and who are better adapted to "market" realities will reap the benefits. This managerial paradigm permeates the mission and all activities of the apostolic centers. Having "flexibility" and "mobility" also allows the Church to operate everywhere and in any circumstances, thereby transcending the local character of the Christian community.

Through his work, Caron aspires to help other churches move from a "rigid structure" to this new apostolic model. The lead apostle of Le Chemin apostolic center hopes to see apostolic teams deployed throughout Canada so that the entire country would participate in a "spiritual revolution in the nations."

The vision proposed by New Apostolic Reformation leaders results from an anachronistic reading of the book of Acts. These modern-day apostles transpose an idealized view of the early Christian communities in Jerusalem, Antioch, Ephesus, Corinth, and Rome to modern times. Their hermeneutic is indifferent to the historical depth separating biblical text from today's experience, and neglects developments (in matters of doctrine, practice, etc.) which have taken place in Christian churches over the centuries.

In reading some of the works dedicated to this apostolic model, it becomes apparent that apostolic centers are presented in two ways, with a constant shift between the two: (1) centers founded by a 1st-century apostle; and (2) "Charismatic" centers founded by a 21st-century apostle. This equivocation serves as a way to legitimize their 21st-century centers by attributing authority to what they interpret to be so-called centers founded by New Testament apostles. In this dual usage, the authors never reveal the differences between these two types of centers and prefer leaving some ambiguity regarding the term "apostle."

Proponents of this modern-day apostolic model place the first of such centers in Jerusalem,[22] led by James the Just. There, apostles were charged with training believers and with managing community property (see Acts 2.42–47; 4.32–35; 5.42). After a time of persecution, many believers left Jerusalem to settle in other regions of Judea and Samaria (see Acts 8.1–4). The book of Acts then provides details of a supposed second apostolic center located in Antioch (Acts 11), which would become a sort of hub for the Apostle Paul's missionary trips.[23] According to this contemporary reading, Ephesus[24] and Corinth[25] would also have been apostolic centers where Christians encountered important challenges with respect to immorality, idolatry, and spiritual antagonism to the Gospel message. As for Rome, it would have been the apostolic center *par excellence*, set at the heart of Roman power and striving to conquer its sociopolitical structures (see Acts 27–28 and the Epistle to the Romans).[26] This type of reading interprets each significant place mentioned in the book of Acts as the deployment of an apostolic center.

The transition from church to apostolic center promises to revive local churches—an attractive aspect for those aspiring to participate in the dynamic power of evangelization and to reinfuse life into a lukewarm congregation. Incitement to dominion transits through to the imperative of the mission and the collective renewal of spiritual life. But for the Church and its members to be fully realized, it would be necessary to accept an important change in the way the Church operates. It would mean to accept that "the Holy Spirit appoint these elders/pastors ... by an Apostle"[27]—i.e., they should no longer be chosen by the assembly. Accepting the apostolic center model amounts to granting total power to the apostle, shattering the (often minimal) democratic practices which characterize evangelical congregations.

Apostolic Centers and Their Territorial Expansion

To achieve their full potential, apostolic centers must be linked to "apostolic networks" allowing them to cover a larger "territory." This approach is counter-intuitive for evangelical churches which, unlike parishes, see themselves as closed communities rather than as part of a territorial subdivision.

> [T]he rest of the account of the book of Acts is a description of the birthing of geographical communities of believers that were linked together into apostolic networks. [...] [T]rue apostolic centres were formed that had a strong influence that reached beyond their own borders. Corinth and Ephesus are examples of this, or even Thessalonica that became a model to all the believers in the provinces of Macedonia and Achaia.
>
> Today the times have changed, but the original pattern is still relevant. Having local churches become apostolic centres, linked together through 21st century apostles and their teams, presents the most potent framework for sustaining the end-time activation of the kingdom dynamics. Just as the seven mountains that influence society are not stand-alone hills, apostolic centres cannot afford the luxury of existing independently from one another. Having a global vision is one of the characteristics of apostles, and apostolic centres must carry that same DNA.[28]

Promoters of this new ecclesial model believe that the Christian communities at Corinth, Ephesus, and Thessalonica were apostolic centers whose influence extended across the Roman Empire. In making "apostolic centers" a central feature of their account, Caron and other leaders of the New Apostolic

Reformation manufacture and rewrite their own new history of the book of Acts. They succeed, to a certain extent, in innovating and justifying their model of apostolic governance by presenting it as a "biblical" model. According to this reading, the apostles Paul and Barnabas worked at creating links between different communities with the goal of achieving greater territorial expansion.

The idea of "territoriality" or "spheres" of apostolic authority is clearly injected into the story of the book of Acts. "Territorial engagement" as a concept was introduced by Bob Beckett[29] during the fourth meeting of the Spiritual Warfare Network (SWN),[30] in 1992 in Pasadena, California.[31] Some years later, in 1996, David Cannistraci, senior pastor of Gateway City Church in San Jose, California, suggested the idea that New Testament apostles each had their own sphere of operation, and that they were responsible for specific boundaries and territories. Cannistraci argued that Barnabas and Saul (who later was named "Paul") were called by the Holy Spirit as apostles (Acts 13.1–3),[32] where each apostle would exercise complete authority within clearly delineated regions. Those who had a spiritual mandate over a territory determined by God were careful not to transgress the boundaries of their apostolate or to interfere in an area where they had not been called. An apostle's authority within his sphere of operation would be comparable to that of an ambassador named by a head of state. According to Cannistraci, the apostles, under the guidance of the Spirit, would have divided various regions with the goal of being uniformly deployed across various geographic areas.[33] The apostles were also tasked with managing conflicts and maintaining order, resolving doctrinal disputes, issuing decrees, naming deacons and elders, and delegating authority to leaders under their apostolic governance.[34] In all these cases, this type of interpretation seeks to legitimize the New Apostolic Reformation's innovative style of apostolic governance by means of an anachronistic reading of the text.

Leaders of the New Apostolic Reformation see the transition from the traditional structure of the local church to that of apostolic centers as a manifestation of the presence of the Kingdom of God in the world. Chuck Pierce,[35] a prophet and the president of Glory of Zion International Ministries[36] and Global Spheres Inc.,[37] believes that one must distinguish between the Kingdom and the Church. The Kingdom becomes a tangible reality through the people who assemble as the Church* and who are subjects of the Kingdom and are called to do its work.[38] The establishment of apostolic centers is thereby linked to the advancement of God's Kingdom here and now, in these last moments before the end times. The distinction between the Church and the Kingdom is as follows: the Church is the community of believers turned in on itself, surviving through generations, while the Kingdom manifests itself when the Church is propelled outside of its walls, busy with conquering the "Seven Mountains" of culture.

The hegemonic language of the "Seven Mountain Mandate" is sometimes disguised by its promoters who feel that the idea is often presented in an alarmist tone by mainstream media.[39] Lance Wallnau, Johnny Enlow,[40] and Os Hillman[41] believe that it is important to use appropriate language according to the understanding of the intended audience.[42] In so doing, they engage in a public relations operation—trading "dominion" for "influence"—while still expecting the same result. Wallnau prefers to avoid references to "conquest" and "dominionism" when addressing the media, this language being reserved for insiders. Wallnau also accuses some conservative Christians of having "apologetic" tendencies which exaggerate and distort the meaning of his message. For Hillman, the "Seven Mountains" strategy is for the purpose of "influence" and is intended as a means to find solutions to contemporary social problems; there is no question of exercising some kind of "domination" over the people. The same is true for Enlow: it is a question of clearly defining what is meant by "dominionism"; if there is dominion, it is one that the light would exert over darkness.[43] Enlow also believes that everyone on earth will rejoice when Christians exercise dominion!

Hillman's concern is with the way in which the mainstream media understands the "Seven Mountain Mandate." He is not troubled by the appeals to biblical war metaphors made by Wallnau and Enlow, inviting Christians to conquer spheres of society. These Christians, drawn to the "Seven Mountains" vision, also willingly accept the vision for "dominion." Hillman does not have misgivings about them; rather, as a good strategist, he seeks to minimize the negative impact that the violent imagery and language of conquest may have on secular people.

What about those who do not share the same ethical values or religious traditions promoted by New Apostolic Reformation leaders? Specifically, when mainstream media report on the "Seven Mountains," they speak from the perspective of the "conquered"—those (believers, agnostics, or atheists) who do not identify with this societal project.[44] The hegemonic vision of the New Apostolic Reformation differs considerably from the values of equality, pluralism, and tolerance characteristic of liberal and democratic societies.[45] To grasp this theology of power, we must now examine some of the networks which uphold it.

Social Transformation through Apostolic Networks

Apostolic networks connect different religious and political entrepreneurs who promote the strategy of conquest and the social, cultural, and political transformation envisioned by the New Apostolic Reformation. Since the founding of Global Spheres Ministries in 1991, Wagner has established many apostolic networks.[46] Some networks have disappeared, some are still active or have been rebranded, and others were created recently. We turn our attention to some of the most significant networks: The International Coalition of Apostolic Leaders and prayer networks such as the One Voice Prayer Movement (OVPM).

International Coalition of Apostolic Leaders (ICAL)

During a meeting in Singapore in 1999, a group of apostles expressed the desire to see the creation of an international network of apostolic leaders. ICAL[47] was founded by Apostle John Kelly later that same year. In 2001, Kelly invited Wagner to take on the role of Presiding Apostle, a position he held until 2009. Kelly resumed apostolic leadership of ICAL in 2010, a role which he has to this day. In addition to founding ICAL, Kelly is the president of the board of directors of Lead Global 360°, an organization dedicated to training Christian entrepreneurs. He is also founder and president of John P. Kelly Ministries, Inc.[48]

Boasting some 2000 apostolic members[49] across more than 85 nations,[50] ICAL's mission is to link all these apostles. The aim of this strategic effort is to establish the Kingdom of God in all aspects of society,[51] which corresponds to implementing the "Seven Mountains" strategy worldwide. The most influential visionary of this social transformation project, Lance Wallnau, is a member of the national council of the United States Coalition of Apostolic Leaders (USCAL), the American branch of ICAL. Members of this board are the movement's top ambassadors, working in conjunction with USCAL's executive team to develop strategies for advancing God's Kingdom in the United States.[52]

As an apostolic network, ICAL also nurtures strategic alliances, serving to transform nations, by means of national apostolic coalitions. There are eight strategic partnerships mentioned on the ICAL website. The following are some examples. Pure Flix, a Christian enterprise pitching itself as an alternative to Netflix, assures an influential role over the "mountains" of religion, family, arts, and education.[53] Lead Global 360° targets the business world[54] with a commitment to training Christian entrepreneurs, and GoStrategic is an international nonprofit organization dedicated to providing Christian leaders with a "biblical education," preparing them to be involved in different areas of society.[55] Among GoStrategic's initiatives is The Statesmen Project,[56] whose work is to train leaders in business, politics, and the media.

The network structure of ICAL is relatively flexible and does not function like a denomination. The ICAL model can be easily reproduced within the associated apostolic networks, which are established on a relational basis rather than an institutional one. Moreover, these networks are difficult to identify and can operate under the radar, without anyone being able to grasp the full extent of their presence and influence.[57] Apostolic prayer networks are a striking example of groups that operate incognito, while still wielding considerable influence.

Apostolic Prayer Networks

Apostolic prayer networks originated as an outgrowth of the SWN.[58] In the early 1990s, Wagner entrusted the American branch of SWN to Cindy Jacobs. This prophetess transformed the group into a prayer and activism network, present in all 50 states, renaming it the United States Spiritual Warfare Prayer Network (USSPN).[59] Jacobs was born in the United States in 1951. Her father was a Southern Baptist minister. (Southern Baptists make up the largest evangelical denomination in the country.) In 1985, Jacobs founded the Generals of Intercession. Recognized for her prophetic ministry, Jacobs still plays an active role at the heart of apostolic prayer networks.[60] In 2008, Jacobs relaunched the SWN under a new guise—the Reformation Prayer Network (RPN)—which is still very active in the United States.[61] Jacobs conceived her prayer and activism network as a catalyst "to bring change to the following areas of societal influence: Religion, Family, Education, Government, Media, Arts & Entertainment and Business."[62] The network thus implements the "Seven Mountains" strategy.

Some of the State Prayer Generals who are part of Cindy Jacobs' RPN are also active members of the Congressional Prayer Caucus Foundation (CPCF).[63] It is important to understand that the CPCF is more than a simple prayer network. This organization strives to "restore and promote America's founding spirit and core principles related to faith and morality by equipping and mobilizing a national network of citizens, legislators, pastors, business owners and opinion leaders," as well as "to protect religious freedom, preserve Judeo-Christian heritage in the United States and promote prayer."[64]

The Heartland Apostolic Prayer Network (HAPN) is another important consortium in the United States. This network, under the leadership of Apostle John Benefiel, is likewise represented in all 50 states. Benefiel founded Oklahoma City's Church on the Rock in 1991.[65] He is also the First Vice-President of Church on the Rock International, an apostolic network comprising more than 6000 churches around the world.[66] HAPN's mission is to see the mountains "of Religion, Family, Education, Government, Media/Arts and Entertainment, Protect & Serve, and Economy in America and the Nations impacted by the Kingdom of God through our prayers and influence."[67] In fact, part of HAPN's activity is dedicated to influence of the "Seven Mountains," through an initiative called Kingdom Culture[68] where "specialists in the culture of the Kingdom" each have responsibility for one of these cultural spheres. The person responsible for HAPN's Kingdom Culture initiative is Yolanda McCune, pastor of a church in Stillwater, Oklahoma, which is also a member congregation of Church on the Rock International.[69]

Among the HAPN networks is the Global Apostolic Prayer Network (GAPN), which has the same goal as HAPN, but its scope is transnational. GAPN is led by Apostle Abby Abildness, who, with her husband James, founded Healing Tree International (HTI), an organization "committed to bringing global solutions to heal and restore the God-ordained destiny of people and nations in collaboration with affiliate networks."[70] This prayer network now extends to some 112 countries.[71] Abildness is also responsible for the Pennsylvania CPCF and is part of Cindy Jacobs' RPN. She also assumes an important role at the center of HAPN as regional leader for the states of Pennsylvania, New Jersey, Delaware, New York, and Maryland.[72]

These apostolic prayer networks are not trivial groups. Each state has its own chapter which depends on the authority of an apostle. These spiritual warriors are not merely content to pray. They produce and distribute literature to inform Christians of significant political issues so as to assure that good candidates—promoted by the Christian right—are elected. These networks also sponsor various events with the goal of bringing together evangelicals and different religious and political figures associated with the New Apostolic Reformation.[73] These prayer networks thereby serve the purpose of political mobilization.

A Prayer Network Tackling Politics

A new prayer network called the OVPM[74] was launched on November 5, 2019. This initiative was that of Paula White-Cain, Trump's former spiritual advisor in the White House and head of the Faith and Opportunity initiative at the White House Office of Public Liaison since November 2019.[75]

White-Cain converted to evangelical faith at the age of 18, claiming she had a vision instructing her to preach Christ's Gospel throughout the world.[76] She briefly attended National Bible College and Seminary in Maryland. Despite not completing her theological studies, she was nonetheless ordained and could preach in Pentecostal churches. Today, White-Cain is an author and televangelist and is often associated with preaching the prosperity gospel.[77] White-Cain produces and hosts a Christian broadcast, *Paula Today*, and short media segments titled *Faithfully with Jon and Paula* with her spouse, Jonathan Cain, former keyboardist of the band Journey. White-Cain is now in her third marriage. She was senior pastor of New Destiny Christian Center, a non-denominational, multi-ethnic mega-church in Apopka, Florida, from 2014 until May 2019.[78]

As Trump's spiritual advisor, White-Cain claims to have led the former president to salvation.[79] She also organized a private meeting between Trump and various evangelical leaders at Trump Tower on September 28, 2015, while he was a Republican Party candidate.[80] Trump was an unconventional contender who claimed not to be part of the political establishment and White-Cain, who is not always accepted in evangelical circles, shares a similar reputation.[81] For example, Russell D. Moore, an influential Southern Baptist leader, had this to say in a tweet about her: "Paula White is a charlatan, recognized as a heretic by every orthodox Christian, of whatever tribe."[82] During the September 28, 2015, meeting, White-Cain nevertheless succeeded in rallying evangelical leaders of various Christian allegiances, and different racial and ethnic backgrounds,[83] such as televangelists Gloria and Kenneth Copeland,[84] pastors Robert Jeffress,[85] Jentezen Franklin,[86] Mark Burns,[87] and Darrell C. Scott,[88] as well as Lance Wallnau[89] among many others.

This venture marked the beginning of White-Cain's politico-religious career. The televangelist would soon be propelled to the forefront of the political scene, notably becoming the first woman to give the invocation prayer for a presidential inauguration ceremony at Trump's 2016 inaugural. Since then, White-Cain has been the primary link between Trump and the evangelicals, giving her the leverage and credibility to launch the OVPM network. Thanks to White-Cain, since 2015, a succession of representatives from different apostolic networks have visited the White House. During the creation of OVPM, White-Cain surrounded herself with various prayer network leaders, among them Mike and Cindy Jacobs, responsible for the Generals of Intercession and the RPN. White-Cain has also reached out to Jon and Jolene Hamill who, for many years, were members of John Benefiel's HAPN and Cindy Jacobs' RPN. Today the Hamills lead Lamplighter Ministries, an organization aligned with Chuck Pierce's apostolic network, Global Spheres. Since 2016, they have also assumed control of Prayer Storm, a worldwide movement founded by James Goll.[90] White-Cain has also invited Dave Kubal,[91] Dutch Sheets,[92] James Goll,[93] and Todd Lamphere[94] to be part of the OVPM team.

OVPM's mission was to unite with "one voice" in prayer on "national issues which are important to God in the United States." These issues were important for Charismatics who supported Trump, and for the Christian right in general: banning abortion, opposition to LGBTQ+ rights, safeguarding "religious liberty," etc. The objective of such a mobilization is for God's divine will to be done "on earth as it is in heaven" (Matt. 6.10). OVPM has converted this phrase from the Our Father prayer into a political slogan.[95] The network clearly served as a political tool for establishing a Christian hegemony in the United States. According to prophet James Goll, Christians found themselves at a crossroads: they were responsible for carrying through this God-given turnaround by securing Trump's presidency, and for assuring that the country would function under a constitutional governance which clearly incorporates biblical values. With White-Cain at the head of OVPM, Charismatics had an unparalleled opportunity.[96] They had succeeded in deploying a network at the very heart of American power, inside the White House, allowing them to influence the president's policies in an unprecedented way—a president who owes his election to white evangelical voters.

According to the Christian Broadcasting Network (CBN), the OVPM was established to combat spiritual opposition that posed a threat to President Trump. This prayer network sought to bring about social transformation by freeing secular society from demonic forces. The Charismatic group involved in this network believed that they were chosen by God to fight against these demonic spirits that hindered the spread of the Gospel message. Such a social transformation project should be a concern for both believers and non-believers, including evangelicals who do not support these religious or political views.

Notes

1 Wagner (1999, pp. 32–53).
2 Wagner (2004, pp. 7–22).
3 See the definition provided by the International Coalition of Apostolic Leaders (ICAL): https://www.icaleaders.com/apostles-today (accessed 22 May 2023).
4 Wagner (2006a, p. 27).
5 See Ahn (2019, pp. 79–83).
6 Wagner (2010, pp. 214 and 280–281).
7 See Wagner (2006a, pp. 77–80). One distinguishes "vertical function apostles" from those with a "horizontal function." The latter are characterized by their gift for developing network connections between apostles, hence the notion of horizontality.
8 The "prophets" receive God's words and revelations which lead them to collaborate with the "apostles" in communicating the content of these revelations. See Wagner (2000a, pp. 98–99).
9 Wagner (2000a, p. 8); (2006a, p. 13); see also Ahn (2019).
10 "... built on the foundation of the apostles and prophets, with Christ Jesus himself as the chief cornerstone" (Eph. 2.20).
11 According to one reading of 1 Corinthians 14.12: "So it is with you. Since you are eager for gifts of the Spirit, try to excel in those that build up the church."
12 Wallnau (2010, pp. 186–187).
13 Wagner (2006b); see also Silvoso (2017).
14 Transliteration of the Greek term ὁδός, meaning "path," "way," or "road."
15 Caron (2013). Caron's book was followed by Pierce and Heidler's (2015).
16 In the following pages, we summarize the content of the HODOS apostolic network. See https://hodos.ca/?lang=en/ (accessed 22 May 2023). [English version – trans.]
17 https://hodos.ca/an-apostolic-blueprint-for-the-21st-century/?lang=en/ (accessed 22 May 2023).
18 Caron (2013, p. 85).
19 See Pierce and Heidler (2015, pp. 63–70).
20 https://hodos.ca/an-apostolic-blueprint-for-the-21st-century/?lang=en/ (accessed 22 May 2023).
21 For a more thorough treatment, see Gonzalez (2014, pp. 332–344).
22 Caron (2013, pp. 144–146) and Pierce and Heidler (2015, pp. 122–128).
23 Caron (2013, pp. 146–152) and Pierce and Heidler (2015, pp. 129–135).

24 Caron (2013, pp. 165–175) and Pierce and Heidler (2015, pp. 136–142).
25 Pierce and Heidler (2015, pp. 143–152).
26 Pierce and Heidler (2015, pp. 153–161).
27 https://hodos.ca/an-apostolic-blueprint-for-the-21st-century/?lang=en/ (accessed 23 May 2023).
28 *Ibid.*
29 Beckett is the senior pastor of Dwelling Place Family Church in the town of Hemet, California. See http://www.dpcitychurch.com/home/ (accessed 23 May 2023).
30 The Spiritual Warfare Network (SWN) was founded by C. Peter Wagner in 1990 (Wagner, 2010, p. 165). It is a network of practitioners dedicated to the study and implementation of the principles of spiritual warfare. We will return to the concept of spiritual warfare in the next chapter. Note that in 2000, SWN became the Apostolic Strategic Prayer Network; see Holvast (2009, p. 144).
31 See Holvast (2009, pp. 100–101).
32 Acts 13.1–3: "[1] Now in the church at Antioch there were prophets and teachers: Barnabas, Simeon called Niger, Lucius of Cyrene, Manaen (who had been brought up with Herod the tetrarch) and Saul.[2] While they were worshiping the Lord and fasting, the Holy Spirit said, 'Set apart for me Barnabas and Saul for the work to which I have called them.'[3] So after they had fasted and prayed, they placed their hands on them and sent them off."
33 Cannistraci (1996, pp. 69–70 and 154).
34 Cannistraci (1996, pp. 155–156).
35 For more details on Chuck Pierce, see Fer and Gonzalez (2017, p. 403).
36 https://gloryofzion.org/ (accessed 23 May 2023).
37 Global Spheres Ministries was founded by C. Peter Wagner in 1991 and reprised by Chuck Pierce in 2010. The organization was initially known as Global Harvest Ministries and was dedicated to the teaching of spiritual warfare and to the mission of socio-cultural transformation; see https://globalspheres.org/ (accessed 23 May 2023).
38 Pierce and Heidler (2015, pp. 9–17).
39 Gonzalez deciphers the controversy around the hegemonic language of the "Seven Mountains" strategy; see Gonzalez (2014, pp. 318–322).
40 Johnny Enlow is senior pastor and founder of Daystar International Christian Fellowship in Atlanta. He leads RESTORE7, a Christian organization which has the goal of enacting reform across the "Seven Mountains" of culture; see https://www.restore7.org/ (accessed 23 May 2023).
41 Hillman worked at his own publicity agency from 1984 to 2001. The agency won many prestigious awards from the direct marketing industry. Today he is founder and president of the Christian organization Marketplace Leaders; see https://www.marketplaceleaders.org/ (accessed 23 May 2023).
42 See the conversation between Wallnau, Enlow, and Hillman: https://www.youtube.com/watch?v=gxTdjFizT9Q/ (accessed 23 May 2023).
43 Johnny Enlow has nonetheless dedicated a great deal of energy to promotion of "Seven Mountains," writing three books on the subject (2008; 2009; 2015). In his last book, he says that it is not about domination, but about influence (2015, pp. 43–54).
44 See Gonzalez for an insightful analysis (2014, pp. 320–321).
45 See André Gagné « Qui sont les évangéliques et comment influencent-ils les élections? », *La Conversation Canada*, 4 December 2018: https://theconversation.com/qui-sont-les-evangeliques-et-comment-influencent-ils-les-elections-106145/ (accessed 23 May 2023).
46 Here are some apostolic networks mentioned by Holvast (2009, p. 160), Wagner (2010, pp. 209–217), Weaver (2016, p. 88) and Christerson and Flory (2017):

New Apostolic Roundtable; Eagles Vision Apostolic Team; Apostolic Council for Educational Accountability; Apostolic Council for Prophetic Elders; and International Coalition of Apostles.

47 The original 1999 organization was the International Coalition of Apostles. It was not until 2013 that the name was changed to the International Coalition of Apostolic Leaders; see https://www.icaleaders.com/about-ical/history-of-ica/ (accessed 23 May 2023).

48 See https://www.johnpkelly.org/biography1/ (accessed 23 May 2023).

49 In June 2023, during a USCAL Bridge Summit, Kelly said that ICAL now has some 2000 members and is present in 87 nations; see: https://youtu.be/2495lFhXiGA (accessed 1 August 2023). There were about 400 members in 2017 according to Christerson and Flory (2017, p. 31).

50 https://www.icaleaders.com/nations/ (accessed 23 May 2023).

51 https://www.icaleaders.com/about-ical/mission-structure/ (accessed 23 May 2023).

52 https://www.uscal.us/council-members/ (accessed 23 May 2023).

53 https://www.pureflix.com/ (accessed 23 May 2023).

54 https://leadglobal360.com/ (accessed 23 May 2023).

55 https://www.gostrategic.org/ (accessed 23 May 2023).

56 https://thestatesmenproject.org/ (accessed 23 May 2023).

57 Weaver (2016, p. 116).

58 There are a panoply of apostolic networks and it is impossible for us to mention them all; see note 46 above as well as the list of resources compiled by Rachel Tabachnick: "Resource Directory for the New Apostolic Reformation," http://www.talk2action.org/story/2010/1/20/131544/037/ (accessed 23 May 2023).

59 Holvast (2009, p. 106).

60 See https://www.generals.org/ (accessed 23 May 2023).

61 Wagner (2010, p. 281).

62 https://www.generals.org/history/ (accessed 23 May 2023).

63 Actually, Mark Hawkins (Alabama), Debra Pratt (Illinois), and Abby Abildness (Pennsylvania) are responsible for their respective states in the two networks; see https://www.generals.org/state-prayer-generals/ (accessed 17 May 2020), as well as: https://cpcfoundation.com/join-the-movement-in-your-state/ (accessed 23 May 2023).

64 https://cpcfoundation.com/about/mission/ (accessed 23 May 2023).

65 https://www.cotr.tv/staff/ (accessed 23 May 2023).

66 http://www.cotri.org/home.html/ (accessed 17 May 2020).

67 https://www.hapn.us/about/ (accessed 23 May 2023).

68 https://hapn.us/hapn-kingdom-culture/ (accessed 23 May 2023).

69 https://www.cotri.org/cotri-church-directory.html/ (accessed 17 May 2020).

70 https://www.healingtreeinternational.com/ (accessed 23 May 2023).

71 https://www.healingtreeinternational.com/gapn/ (accessed 23 May 2023).

72 https://www.hapn.us/hapn-united-states/ (accessed 23 May 2023).

73 Rachel Tabachnick, "Spiritual Warriors with an Antigay Mission: The New Apostolic Reformation": https://www.politicalresearch.org/2013/03/22/spiritual-warriors-with-an-antigay-mission/ (accessed 23 May 2023).

74 James Goll, "Cindy Jacobs, Paula White Cain, Dutch Sheets Launching New Governmental Prayer Initiative": https://www.charismanews.com/opinion/78684-cindy-jacobs-paula-white-cain-dutch-sheets-launching-new-governmental-prayer-initiative/ (accessed 23 May 2023).

75 Jeremy W. Peters and Elizabeth Dias, "Paula White, Newest White House Aide, Is a Uniquely Trumpian Pastor": https://www.nytimes.com/2019/11/02/us/politics/paula-white-trump.html/ (accessed 23 May 2023).

76 https://paulawhite.org/paula.html#news1-25/ (accessed 23 May 2023).

77 According to prosperity gospel preachers, there is a link between one's intensity of faith, physical well-being, financial success, and spiritual victory; see Bowler (2013, pp. 249–262).

78 Carol Kuruvilla, "Paula White, Trump's Spiritual Adviser, Leaves Florida Church With New Ambitions": https://www.huffpost.com/entry/paula-white-trump-church_n_5cd2e310e4b0a7dffccfa91e/ (accessed 23 May 2023).

79 Julia Duin, "She led Trump to Christ: The rise of the televangelist who advises the White House": https://www.washingtonpost.com/lifestyle/magazine/she-led-trump-to-christ-the-rise-of-the-televangelist-who-advises-the-white-house/2017/11/13/1dc3a830-bb1a-11e7-be94-fabb0f1e9ffb_story.html (accessed 23 May 2023).

80 Ben Schreckinger, "Donald Trump's saving grace: Televangelists": https://www.politico.com/story/2015/09/donald-trumps-evangelicals-televangelists-214250/ (accessed 23 May 2023).

81 See article by Michael Horton, professor of theology at Westminster Seminary in California, "Evangelicals should be deeply troubled by Donald Trump's attempt to mainstream heresy": https://www.washingtonpost.com/news/acts-of-faith/wp/2017/01/03/evangelicals-should-be-deeply-troubled-by-donald-trumps-attempt-to-mainstream-heresy/ (accessed 23 May 2023).

82 https://twitter.com/drmoore/status/747803028661669888/ (accessed 23 May 2023).

83 See https://gothamist.com/news/video-trump-presidency-secured-with-closed-door-prayer-ceremony/ (accessed 23 May 2023).

84 Well known in the United States, Kenneth Copeland and his wife Gloria preach the "prosperity gospel." They lead Kenneth Copeland Ministries, an organization located in Fort Worth, Texas; see https://www.kcm.org/ (accessed 23 May 2023).

85 As we will see in Chapter 3, Robert Jeffress is an important ally of Donald Trump. He is also senior pastor of the First Baptist Church in Dallas; see https://www.firstdallas.org (accessed 23 May 2023).

86 Jentezen Franklin is senior pastor of the multi-campus Free Chapel church, based in Gainesville, Georgia; see https://www.freechapel.org/about/ (accessed 23 May 2023).

87 Mark Burns is an African American pastor responsible for the Harvest Praise & Worship Center in South Carolina; see https://www.cbsnews.com/news/why-some-african-american-evangelicals-are-playing-the-trump-card/ (accessed 23 May 2023).

88 Darrell C. Scott is cofounder of New Spirit Revival Center, in Cleveland Heights, Ohio. He was also one of the first African American pastors to support Trump in 2016. He and Trump lawyer Michael D. Cohen founded the National Diversity Coalition for Trump: https://www.cleveland.com/open/2015/11/cleveland_heights_pastor_darre.html (accessed 18 May 2020).

89 Wallnau wrote two accounts of his impressions of the September 28, 2015, meeting with Trump; see https://lancewallnau.com/meeting-donald-trump-an-insiders-report/#more-14633/ (accessed 23 May 2023), and https://lancewallnau.com/trump-tells-us-more/#more-14627/ (accessed 23 May 2023).

90 See https://www.facebook.com/jonandjolene/ (accessed 23 May 2023).

91 Dave Kubal is president of Intercessors for America; see https://ifapray.org/ (accessed 23 May 2023).

92 Dutch Sheets is a Christian author and speaker working to reform American society for a radical awakening; see https://dutchsheets.org/index.php/about/ (accessed 23 May 2023).

93 James Goll is president of God Encounters Ministries and is part of the apostolic team of Harvest International Ministries; see https://godencounters.com/james-w-goll-bio/ (accessed 23 May 2023).

94 Todd Lamphere works in collaboration with Paula White. He is the top pastor of Paula White Ministries Global Outreach; see https://www1.cbn.com/cbnnews/us/2018/november/what-are-conditions-really-like-in-governments-tent-city-for-immigrant-youth-ndash-and-how-can-churches-serve-them/ (accessed 23 May 2023).

95 See https://onevoiceprayermovement.com/ (accessed 18 May 2020).

96 Peter Montgomery, "Paula White's One Voice Prayer Movement: A Thinly Disguised Political Operation for Trump": https://www.rightwingwatch.org/post/paula-whites-one-voice-prayer-movement-a-thinly-disguised-political-operation-for-trump/ (accessed 23 May 2023).

3

SPIRITUAL WARFARE AND THE SPECTER OF CIVIL WAR

According to some of the Charismatic leaders who supported Trump, the United States is embroiled in spiritual warfare against evil invisible forces who sought to undermine the former president and his work. These demonic forces were believed to have acted primarily through Trump's political adversaries. For a great majority of the American population and the mainstream media, the idea of spiritual warfare is an exotic concept difficult to grasp. Nonetheless, due to the popularity of some Charismatics close to the former president, spiritual warfare sometimes makes headlines, eliciting strong reactions from readers of mainstream media.

One of the most vocal advocates of spiritual warfare is Paula White-Cain. There are two significant moments where we have witnessed her engagement in spiritual warfare. As we will see, these two episodes showcase the reception of this idea both in mainstream media and by a segment of the American population.

The Polarizing Rhetoric of Spiritual Warfare

The rhetoric of spiritual warfare contributes to the current political and social polarization seen in the United States. It comes as no surprise that the media and those who do not share the faith and point of view of Charismatics react negatively to such a worldview. Moreover, the language of spiritual warfare is sometimes difficult to decipher, and only "insiders" seem to understand some of the cryptic expressions that are used. One striking example is that of a spiritual warfare prayer by Paula White-Cain in her Florida church, City of Destiny, during a meeting on January 5, 2020[1]:

DOI: 10.4324/9781003358718-4

We interrupt that which has been deployed to hurt the Church in this season, that which has been deployed to hurt this nation, in the name of Jesus. Forgive us! —for our sins—*Come on, I need you guys to pray!*— We cancel every surprise from the witchcraft and the marine kingdom. Any hex, any spell, any witchcraft, any spirit of control, any Jezebel. Anything that the enemy desires through spells, through witchcraft, through any way that is manipulation, demonic manipulation, we curse that. We break it, according to the Word of God, in the name of Jesus. We come against the marine kingdom. We come against the animal kingdom. The woman that rides upon the waters. We break the power, in the name of Jesus. And we declare that any strange winds, any strange winds that have been sent to hurt the Church, sent against this nation, sent against our president, sent against myself, sent against others, we break it by the superior blood of Jesus right now. In the name of Jesus, we arrest every infirmity, affliction, fatigue, weariness, weakness, fear, sickness, any self-righteousness, any self-serving action, God. Let pride fall! Let pride fall! Let pride fall! Let pride fall! In the name of Jesus, we command all satanic pregnancies to miscarry right now! We declare that anything that's been conceived in satanic wombs, that it will miscarry, it will not be able to carry forth any plan of destruction, any plan of harm.[2]

Reactions were swift, particularly to her reference to "satanic pregnancies." Well-known Jesuit priest James Martin fired back, saying: "No pregnancies are satanic. Every child is a gift from God. No one should ever pray for any woman to miscarry."[3] The debate took a different turn when Jennifer Gunter, an obstetrician and gynecologist writing for the *New York Times*, retorted: "So Paula White wants everyone at the White House to know she is praying for abortion."[4] Costi W. Hinn, a pastor at Redeemer Bible Church in Arizona, also brought it back to the question of abortion, saying:

So we are against abortion and consider it the murder of a baby, except when Paula White commands that someone miscarry? What if that 'Satanic' little baby gets a revelation of the grace of God one day? Lord have mercy.[5]

We note that although Costi Hinn is the nephew of celebrated American preacher Benny Hinn, he does not share any of his uncle's beliefs, nor those of White-Cain. Representatives of the Church of Satan also weighed in, suggesting it was insensitive of White-Cain to pray for the abortion of pregnancies without the consent of the women involved.[6] Others claimed that White-Cain was asking God to abort the babies of Trump's enemies.[7] All the reactions had the same take: Paula White-Cain was asking that God abort the pregnancies of non-believers or of Trump's opponents because their offspring would be "satanic." The comments focused on the question of "satanic pregnancies," forgetting the context in which the prayer had been expressed.

To associate Satan with miscarriage is certainly not a judicious idea on White-Cain's part, particularly at a time when the debate over women's reproductive rights was raging in the United States. It was not surprising that her statements raised the ire of those who do not understand such obscure language. The controversial clip was a brief excerpt from a prayer service taking place in the preacher's own church before an audience familiar with spiritual warfare jargon. White-Cain responded to critics, explaining that the words had been taken out of context and that she was referring to Ephesians 6.12, and she accused her critics of being dishonest, seeking merely to obtain political gain.[8] We will return to the importance of Ephesians 6.12 in the next section of this chapter.

Without making any excuses for White-Cain, her words were misinterpreted. The reference to "satanic pregnancies" must first be placed in the context of this specific spiritual warfare prayer. White-Cain begins her prayer by asking that a demonic power which has been deployed to hurt the Church and the nation be stopped. She then asks God to forgive the sins of everyone present and decrees an end to all evil resulting from spells, witchcraft, hexes, controlling spirits, Jezebel, and the marine kingdom. Her references to witchcraft are straightforward and easily understandable. We will return to the significance of Jezebel.

But what does White-Cain mean by her reference to the "marine kingdom"? Some Charismatics hold that demonic spirits inhabit the depths of the sea and that believers should engage them in spiritual warfare. Ana Méndez Ferrell,[9] an apostle, prophetess, and the cofounder of an organization called Voice of the Light Ministries in Jacksonville, Florida, has ventured on undersea diving expeditions with prayer teams to engage in battle against the demonic forces acting beneath the waters.[10] Other influential leaders, such as Daniel K. Olukoya,[11] Pat Holliday,[12] and Jennifer LeClaire,[13] have also written books about "marine spirits."[14] As far as that goes, Cindy Jacobs (whom we discussed in the preceding chapter in regard to apostolic networks) has referred to "Leviathan" as a "marine spirit" living in the waters and affecting individuals, nations, and sometimes even the Church.[15] The *Mystery of the Iniquity* website mentions Pat Holliday on the subject of "marine spirits":

> There are rulers and principalities from the sea! And the witches and wizards, who are Satan's agents, understand these powers and submit to them. Spirits from the sea rule countries and cities above the waters, and below. They are governed and occupied these spirits [...] and not everyone can see these places. They are invisible to the physical eye. These cities are considered 'phantasmal.' Phantasm: an apparition or

specter. These creatures can live in more than one dimension. They are very real … as real as you and me. We are wonderfully and beautifully made by GOD but we exist on two levels, as well. We are natural but our spirit is supernatural. Some of these creatures have the ability to live in dual realities too.[16]

This is what Paula White-Cain is referring to when she mentions the "marine kingdom": an invisible, supernatural reality which influences the course of daily life and tries to undermine God's divine will for the Church and for the United States. We can also better understand the significance of "the woman who rides upon the waters" following the second mention of the "marine kingdom" in her spiritual warfare prayer. White-Cain simply assimilates the "spirit of Jezebel" from Revelation 2.20–23 ("Nevertheless, I have this against you: You tolerate that woman Jezebel, who calls herself a prophet. By her teaching she misleads my servants into sexual immorality and the eating of food sacrificed to idols."—Rev. 2.20) to the figure of the whore of Babylon "sitting by many waters" in Revelation 17.1–18; two figures now part of the "marine kingdom."[17]

White-Cain then prays against the "animal kingdom," another metaphor which is difficult to decipher. Some authors go so far as to compare the characteristics of certain animals to the behavior of evil spirits. For example, Jennifer Eivaz[18] claims that the Bible compares the crocodile to Leviathan: "[T]here are attributes that are associated with this sea creature that are also attributes of this spirit prince known as Leviathan."[19] Apostle John Eckhardt, founder of the apostolic network Global Impact and senior pastor of Crusader Church in Chicago, makes the same type of comparison with the ostrich (see Job 39.13–19) and claims that those who do not take care of their children are under the influence of an "ostrich spirit," characterized by a lack of wisdom and hardness of heart.[20] Once again, these metaphors are used in the context of spiritual warfare.

Continuing with her prayer, White-Cain claims to be able to break all "strange wind" seeking to harm the Church, the president, the nation, and the people by the "superior blood of Jesus." The blood of Jesus represents Christ's death, a death which is believed to have destroyed the forces of evil. As to "strange [or contrary] winds," this is likely an appeal for divine protection against the dangers of being tossed around and carried away "by every wind of teaching and by the cunning and craftiness of people in their deceitful scheming" (Eph. 4.14). This is certainly an appeal for divine protection against "false doctrines" that are contrary to her understanding of the Christian message, but the point is also directed toward any manipulation coming from political adversaries.

The most contentious element of this prayer is for all "satanic pregnancies," i.e., those conceived in "satanic wombs," to result in miscarriages. It is this part of her prayer, in particular, which caught media and public attention. As we have mentioned, White-Cain's words were interpreted at face value, as if she appealed to God that non-believing women or those opposed to Trump would suffer miscarriages. A contextual reading of this spiritual warfare prayer shows that this is not the case. We can better understand it as a prayer for protection against Satan's evil plans; the preacher orders that the devil's plans be miscarried. White-Cain expressed ideas familiar to people in Charismatic and Pentecostal circles, which refer to certain texts found in the Bible. For Daniel K. Olukoya, it is necessary to believe that God will not allow the enemy (Satan) to give birth to the evil which is conceived against believers; that God will prevent "satanic pregnancies" from materializing.[21] We note the metaphoric use of pregnancy in connection with the "conception" of evil in certain biblical texts: "[Corrupt man] conceive trouble and give birth to evil; their womb fashions deceit" (Job 15.35); "Whoever is pregnant with evil conceives trouble and gives birth to disillusionment" (Ps. 7.14); "Then, after desire has conceived, it gives birth to sin; and sin, when it is full-grown, gives birth to death" (Jas. 1.15). In each example, the language of pregnancy is symbolic. One can essentially conceive evil in the "womb" and ripen it.

Ultimately, White-Cain's request is not for the abortion of "satanic babies," but for the annihilation or miscarriage of diabolic schemes against all Christians. The bad intentions ascribed to her and the misinterpretation of the meaning of "satanic pregnancies" came from the fact that the mainstream media is accustomed to White-Cain's polarizing rhetoric. We will now examine how White-Cain used spiritual warfare to stigmatize Trump's political adversaries.

Spiritual Warfare and Trump's Enemies

On June 18, 2019, during the launch of Donald Trump's re-election campaign at the Amway Center in Orlando, Florida, Paula White-Cain, in front of a crowd of 20,000 people, engaged in a spiritual warfare prayer to defeat the demonic forces opposed to the president. We will examine an excerpt from this prayer by dividing it into several parts and highlight White-Cain's spiritual warfare rhetoric and her use of it for political ends.

As White-Cain approached the podium where Trump would give his speech, she asked the crowd to stand to participate in the prayer and invited everyone to take their neighbor's hand.[22] The preacher then delivered this prayer:

> Father, I come to you in the name of Jesus, and first and foremost I give you thanks for our great United States. I give you thanks for our president and for your blessings and your goodness. Your Word declares in Psalm Chapter 34, Verse 1, that "I will bless the Lord at all times and his praise

shall continually be in my mouth." So, we thank you and we bless you God, for your goodness, for your grace, for your mercy. I pray for the Spirit of the Lord to rest upon our president and that your favor cause his horn, his power, to be exalted according to Psalm Chapter 89, Verse 17.[23]

White-Cain began her prayer by first thanking the Lord for the great country that is the United States, a nation having been described as privileged, both chosen and blessed by God, and by quoting the first verse of Psalm 34. White-Cain's prayers are characteristically punctuated with biblical quotes—always out of context—that become the framework of the narrative she constructs throughout her petition. This prayer is not only addressed to God but is also aimed at the audience, because White-Cain tells them a story, that of the divine appointment of Donald Trump to the presidency and the spiritual warfare which the forces of evil lead against him. She asks that the Spirit of the Lord rest on Trump and that his "horn"[24] be exalted. The references to the "Spirit of the Lord" and to the "horn" of power inform the audience that Trump is God's chosen one and that he exercises his authority in God's name. But the preacher's plea has only started:

> Lord, your Word says in Psalm Chapter 2, Verse 1 through 4: "Why do the nations conspire, and the peoples plot in vain? The kings of the earth rise up and the rulers band together against the Lord and against his anointed, saying 'let us break their chains and throw off their shackles!' The One enthroned in the heaven laughs; the Lord scoffs at them." Father, you have raised President Trump up for such a time as this. You are a God that reveals secrets. So, reveal the secret and the deep things to President Trump, according to Daniel, Chapter 2, Verse 22. Make known unto him the mystery of your will. [...] Let every evil veil of deception of the enemy be removed from people's eyes, in the name, which is above every name, the name of Jesus Christ![25]

White-Cain quotes verses 1 through 4 of Psalm 2, a messianic psalm about King David, and applies them directly to President Trump. Again, we find the idea, discussed in Chapter 1, of Trump as the modern-day Cyrus: an "anointed one" chosen by God to deliver the United States from the grip of secularism and to annihilate all opposition against Christians. In the biblical context, the author of Psalm 2 reacts to the nations and those who oppose the Lord's "anointed," saying that nothing can change the course of history: God mocks his adversaries, having sovereignly chosen his "anointed." The same would be true for Donald Trump, according to Paula White-Cain, as she claims that God has "raised President Trump up for such a time as this." But for Trump to be able to exercise his political power according to God's divine will, it is necessary to ask that God grant the president the revelation of "secret and deep things," akin to the prayer of the Prophet Daniel.[26] In the context of his re-election, Trump needed a revelation of "secret and deep things" to unmask and dismantle the "Deep State"[27] and the efforts of the Mueller investigation,[28] which together were seeking to destabilize the former president.[29]

The Bible and Spiritual Warfare: Ephesians 6.12

White-Cain's speech becomes more explicit when she mentions the presence of "demonic networks":

> For you've said in your Word—*so I am going to deal with some principalities now, okay?*—because you said in your Word, in Ephesians, Chapter 6, Verse 12, that "we're not wrestling against flesh and blood, but against principalities, powers, against rulers of darkness of this world, against spiritual wickedness in high places." So right now, let every demonic network that has aligned itself against the purpose, against the calling of President Trump, let it be broken, let it be torn down in the name of Jesus! Let the counsel of the wicked be spoiled right now, according to Job, Chapter 12, Verse 17. I declare that President Trump will overcome every strategy from hell, and every strategy of the enemy, every strategy, and he will fulfill his calling and his destiny. Destroy and divide their tongues, O Lord, according to Psalm 55, Verse 9! Give President Trump strength to bring forth his destiny according to Isaiah, Chapter 66, Verse 9! Let the secret counsel of wickedness be turned to foolishness right now, in Jesus' name![30]

It is here that Paula White-Cain engages in warfare prayer, a form of intercessory prayer common in Charismatic circles. Believers resort to this style of prayer in which they engage in a battle against invisible, supernatural entities they deem to be harmful to their personal lives, society, politics, and even to some geographic regions.[31] The goal is to thwart the wiles of evil forces which try to prevent the proclamation of the Gospel message and hinder the expansion of God's Kingdom on earth. As it concerns Trump, White-Cain asked that the veils of deception of the *enemy* "be removed from people's eyes." Clearly, the foremost *enemy* is the devil, as this is a common expression among evangelicals.[32] Simultaneously, as we will later see, a shift of meaning takes place here: the "enemy" can refer implicitly to the "Deep State" and to the Mueller investigation, both harmful to the Trump administration. Note that the prayer is done "in the name of Jesus [Christ]," the name which is "above every name." Praying in this manner is common among evangelicals. In effect, one believes that the prayer will be more powerful if it is directed toward God in the "name of Jesus," which implies that Jesus' authority is transferred to those that follow him.[33]

Following this common formulation, White-Cain addresses the crowd to highlight that she is going to attack "principalities," and this is when she quotes Ephesians 6.12:

We're not wrestling against flesh and blood, but against principalities, powers, against rulers of darkness of this world, against spiritual wickedness in high places.

The idea of spiritual warfare is often legitimized through the use of this popular biblical text; it is a passage cherished among Charismatics who engage in this spiritual practice. In the 1990s, C. Peter Wagner developed a systematic paradigm for spiritual warfare, where he introduced and infused new ways of interpreting certain biblical texts. According to Wagner, believers are caught up in a battle against the forces of evil. These spiritual entities were believed to be responsible for the conflicts between people, problems in daily life, political tensions in the world, etc. Generally speaking, our world would be affected by a spiritual conflict between invisible, but quite real, good and evil forces battling each other. It is believed that Christians, by the power of prayer, were called to neutralize the Machiavellian schemes of these evil forces, but this battle could also be waged through their social and political activism. For these Charismatics, the struggle is not solely against "flesh and blood" (human beings), but also involves demonic forces at work to inspire—and even in some cases possess—people opposed to God's will.

To explain the extent of this invisible conflict between good and evil, Wagner[34] argued that spiritual warfare is manifest at three levels of engagement.[35] He called the first level "ground level spiritual warfare." This level would involve the practice of exorcism, with some individuals having the power to cast out demons. This corresponds to the power which Jesus conferred on his disciples when they were sent on their mission (see Matt. 10.1; Luke 10.17; Acts 8.7). According to Wagner, this "earthly warfare" is the type of activity most commonly mentioned in the New Testament, an undertaking which the author links to most contemporary deliverance ministries.[36]

Wagner also identified a second level, which he called "occult-level spiritual warfare." This realm involves battling demonic powers acting through people who indulge in practices identified—in the evangelical world—as "occult" (shamanism, New Age, yoga, sorcery, satanism, etc.). These forces are not of the same order as the "ordinary" demons responsible for headaches, family conflicts, or alcoholism. For example, Wagner illustrated this type of spiritual conflict with a text from the Acts of the Apostles: the story of the Apostle Paul's political imprisonment following the exorcism of a slave girl with an evil spirit; this exorcism resulted in the loss of her fortune-telling abilities and caused social and political upheaval in the region (see Acts 16.16–24).

Finally, Wagner also spoke of "strategic-level spiritual warfare."[37] This is the level to which Paula White-Cain refers when she appeals to the text of Ephesians 6.12. These Charismatics believe that a hierarchy of high-ranking demonic spirits, mandated by Satan and acting on his behalf, controls nations, regions, cities, tribes, groups of people, and neighborhoods, as well as various important networks around the world. Wagner referred to these entities as "territorial spirits" who oversee the activity of lower ranking demons to prevent God's purpose from prevailing in their territory.[38]

Wagner supported the idea of "strategic-level spiritual warfare" with references to certain biblical texts. While forced to confess that the Bible does not contain "proofs" concerning this type of warfare, Wagner contended that biblical texts still provide enough information to accept the hypothesis of such a reality.[39] For example, the author of the book of Revelation depicts the outbreak of a spiritual war in the heavens, where "Michael and his angels fought against the dragon, and the dragon and his angels fought back" (Rev. 12.7). Wagner believed this depiction of an invisible and spiritual conflict, a fierce battle in the heavens where angels and demons are pitted against one another, to be realistic. As for the territorial character of demonic control, Wagner relied on a passage from the book of Deuteronomy[40]: "When the Most High gave an inheritance to the nations, when he separated the children of men, he set up boundaries for the peoples according to the number of the sons of God" (Deut. 32.8).[41] Wagner also relied on F. F. Bruce, an esteemed evangelical exegete, for his interpretation of this text[42]:

This reading implies that the administration of the various nations has been parceled out among a corresponding number of angelic powers [...]. In a number of places some at least of these angelic governors are portrayed as hostile principalities and powers—the "world rulers of this darkness" of Ephesians 6.12.[43]

Based on this commentary by Bruce, Wagner argued that another biblical passage, from the book of the prophet Daniel, explicitly mentioned what is suggested in Deuteronomy. Chapter 10 of the book of the prophet Daniel gives a spiritual warfare account between three heavenly "princes" or "chief princes." Two among them are understood as evil and hostile entities, "the prince of Persia" and "the prince of Greece"[44] (Dan. 10.13–20); the only good "chief prince" is Michael, described as "one of the chief princes" and responsible for the people of Israel (Dan. 10.21). In this story, an angel sent by God must fight a 21-day battle against the "prince of Persia" in order to reach Daniel with God's message. The angel only succeeds in defeating the "prince of Persia" with Michael's help. For Wagner, this story—which he believed to be factual—sheds light on the power of the "princes of darkness."[45]

This belief that evil spirits occupy geographical spaces and exert territorial influence also relies in part on how Old Testament stories concerning Israel and the divinities of neighboring nations (see Josh. 24.14) are interpreted. In fact, Wagner thought that pagan gods represented territorial spirits controlling people and regions with which they were associated (see 2 Kings 17.30–31). This would explain, according to Wagner, why the nations under the domination of these divinities were susceptible to witchcraft, occultism, and astrology (2 Kings 17.17) and why the Israelites were reprimanded for having neglected to destroy the idols and divination objects of conquered countries (Judg. 3.7).[46]

Likewise, Wagner references several New Testament texts where Jesus and the apostles engage in what he interprets to be "strategic-level spiritual warfare." Some stories from the book of Acts are seen as episodes of spiritual warfare waged between apostles (such as Peter and Paul) and those who opposed the Gospel message. For example, Wagner interprets the confrontation between Peter and Simon the Magician in the town of Samaria (see Acts 8) in those terms. In disarming Simon of his spiritual control over the Samaritans, Peter was attacking a "territorial spirit" which laid claim over the town and paving the way for the conversion of multitudes to the Gospel message.[47]

According to Wagner, an excellent way to visualize this spiritual warfare, where evil spirits fight against the angels of God, is through novels such as *This Present Darkness* and *Piercing the Darkness* by Canadian author Frank E. Peretti.[48] These two novels present graphic depictions of Christians partaking in battles between the supernatural forces of good and evil through "warfare prayer" and by living in step with "Judeo-Christian values." In fact, these novels are theological and apologetic works of fiction. Peretti staged fictitious characters to promote a particular worldview and set of beliefs about spiritual warfare. Even if these novels are fiction, the demonology clearly is not.

Mapping Demonic Activity

If one thinks that these ideas regarding demonology have no impact on daily life, that they are nothing more than abstract concepts from old biblical stories or, at most, only related to the "spiritual" world, think again! For proponents of spiritual warfare, these evil spirits play a role in the political, social, and cultural life of a nation. It is believed that such demonic forces exercise considerable influence on the inhabitants of their territory and hinder the expansion of the Kingdom of God. Publications dedicated to spiritual warfare and to its strategies are replete with contemporary examples of "demonized" countries, regions, cities, political parties, etc., all the while explaining how to carry out "territorial exorcisms" by means of spiritual warfare prayer. But even before attempting to war against demonic principalities, spiritual warfare practitioners must undertake the task of spiritually "mapping" besieged territories.[49] George Otis, Jr., is a pioneer of this practice.[50] He explains "spiritual mapping" as follows:

> In short, we must learn to see the world as it really is, not as it appears to be. This new way of seeing I have labeled *spiritual mapping*. It involves superimposing our understanding of forces and events in the spiritual domain onto places and circumstances in the material world. The result is often a set of borders, capitals and battlefronts that differ notably from those we have come to associate with the political status quo. On this new map of the world the three spiritual superpowers we have examined—Hinduism, materialism, Islam—are not entities in themselves. They are, rather, the *means* by which an extensive hierarchy of powerful demonic authorities controls billions of people.[51]

This quote should be read in the context of Otis, Jr.'s own spiritual mapping work, which led to the publication of his book in 1991. Such work requires the territorial identification of cities recognized as "spiritual capitals" or "besieged cities," as well as the delineation of what is known as the 10/40 Window. This geographic space was first mentioned in 1990 by Christian missionary and strategist Luis Bush. Today, the Joshua Project describes the 10/40 Window as

> the rectangular area of North Africa, the Middle East and Asia approximately between 10 degrees north and 40 degrees north latitude. The 10/40 Window is often called 'The Resistant Belt' and includes the majority of the world's Muslims, Hindus, and Buddhists. The original 10/40 Window included only countries with at least 50% of their land mass within 10 and 40 degrees north latitude. The revised 10/40 Window includes several additional countries that are close to 10 or 40 degrees north latitude and have high concentrations of unreached peoples.[52]

Otis Jr. explained that practitioners of spiritual mapping chart their world map based on the alleged demonic activity which they claim to identify through historical, anthropological, and sociological research of the target regions. Otis Jr. blends this cartographic work with a form of prayer activity which he calls "informed intercession." To better understand what is at stake in each target region (i.e., people's worldviews, ideologies, religious rituals, discourses, and practices, as well as social organizations, ethnic groups, power structures, etc.), Otis Jr. believed that "informed intercession" primarily depends on deep cultural anthropological work.[53] All gathered information must then be interpreted, and it is through the analysis of this data that practitioners claim to discern which demonic forces are at work in each territory (country, city, neighborhood, business, etc.). Once these "evil principalities" have been identified, they can be spiritually confronted through "Prayer Walking," where believers are invited to perform intercessory prayers on site. Prayer groups walk the streets of a neighborhood or town[54] and can go so far as to cover several territories, even large geographical regions.[55]

This spiritual warfare theology creates conditions which lead to the demonization of peoples, cultures, and political communities. A shift occurs when some Charismatics engage in spiritual warfare against demonic forces. Translating from spiritual entities to "flesh and blood" beings (Eph. 6.12), non-believers and political or cultural enemies (Islam, LGBTQ+, etc.) become assimilated into evil spirits. This translation of evil spirits to "flesh and blood" enemies can be seen in White-Cain's prayer—the preacher shifts from fighting "demonic networks" to destroying "the counsel of the wicked," from "strategies of hell and of the enemy" to the destruction of their "evil tongues" and the routing of the "secret counsel of wickedness." Gonzalez has expressly noted this shift from the spiritual to the political.[56] The "demonic networks" and the "secret counsel of wickedness" were also ways of referring to all of Trump's enemies: the mainstream media, the "Deep State," and the Democrats who sought to remove the president following the Mueller investigation. The reaction of media outlets varied. Mainstream media questioned the significance and political implications of White-Cain's words, while *Fox News* and *CBN*, a popular evangelical network, focused on what they believed to be the spiritual meaning conveyed by the preacher's message.

Protecting Trump against His Enemies

At the end of her prayer, White-Cain insisted on former President Trump's need for protection. This is when she "decreed" (a word of authority) to secure the candidate's re-election:

> And I declare that no weapon formed against him, his family, his calling, his purpose, this counsel, will be able to be formed! Now I declare that you will surround him and protect him from all destruction. Let the Angel of the Lord encamp around about him, around his family, according to Psalm Chapter 34, Verse 7. Establish him in righteousness and let oppression be far from him according to Isaiah 54.14. I deploy the hand of God to work for him in the name of Jesus! I secure his calling! I secure his purpose! I secure his family! And we secure victory in the name, which is above every name, the name that has never failed for this nation and for my life, the name of Jesus Christ! And everybody said "Amen!"[57]

She concluded her decree by stating that "no weapon formed against him (Trump), his family, his calling, his purpose, this counsel, will be able to be formed." This idea suggests that supernatural forces are at play in politics, leading to the belief that political opponents and the mainstream media spreading "fake news" about President Trump are under the influence of demonic entities. The preacher decrees divine protection for the president, appealing to the Angel of the Lord to "encamp around about him, around his family"; she "deploys the hand of God to work for him"; she "secures" Trump's calling, his mission, his family, and his victory "in the name of Jesus." The language used by White-Cain indicates that she believes herself to have been given a divine mandate and that she has the authority to decree and exercise power accordingly.[58]

One must be reminded that this prayer was delivered during a rally for Trump's re-election campaign. Throughout White-Cain's prayer, the crowd showed enthusiasm, applauding her several times. She successfully fired up the crowd and created a positive atmosphere for Trump's speech. White-Cain is accustomed to addressing crowds. A few months after the launch of Trump's re-election campaign, White-Cain attended an "Evangelicals for Trump" meeting held in Miami on January 3, 2020. There again she decreed divine protection for Trump, commanding that "no weapon formed against him [the president] will be able to prosper, and that every demonic altar erected against him will be torn down."[59] This time, however, the mainstream media gave more attention to the coalition of evangelicals preparing for Trump's re-election than the specific content White-Cain's prayer.

Other Charismatic Trump supporters also used this type of language. For instance, Lance Wallnau frequently adopted bellicose rhetoric to demonize the Democratic Party. Wallnau commented on the Democrats' reaction to Trump's February 4, 2020, State of the Union speech in these terms: "Christians need to get involved with every sphere: academia, media, entertainment, law, business and politics. WATCH and see a political party under the influence of a spirit that can't celebrate American Prosperity."[60] His mention of spheres is a truncated reference to the "Seven Mountains," but the point he wanted to make is that the Democrats are "under the influence of a spirit." Wallnau used language commonly known among Charismatics to demonize the Democratic Party. If a Party is "under the influence of a spirit that can't celebrate American prosperity," it means that it is under demonic influence and opposed to the divine plan for the United States; it has become an enemy of God. For Wallnau, it follows that a nation's economic health is directly linked to its obedience to God: "You actually have to realize that where the Spirit of the Lord is, there is freedom, and if you want to see freedom economically, or freedom culturally, or freedom politically, you have to honor God."[61] Wallnau believes that those who oppose Trump's economic plan are controlled by demons. How can one oppose American prosperity, which is a sign of divine approval? There is no doubt for Wallnau: the Democratic Party is a demonized political organization.

The POTUS Shield initiative,[62] led by its founder Frank Amedia, is a group of intercessors for the nation who were also concerned with protecting President Trump. Amedia and his wife Lorilee are founders of Touch Heaven Ministries, an international ministry active in multiple countries across Africa and Asia. They also serve as senior pastors of Touch Heaven Church in Canfield, Ohio.[63] Amedia is a regular guest on the *Jim Bakker Show* and engages in the practice of "spiritual gifts." (Recall that the *Jim Bakker Show* is a daily broadcast of Charismatic persuasion focused on biblical prophecies about the end times and the second coming of Christ.) Amedia also served as a liaison between some "prophetic" leaders and Donald Trump during the 2016 presidential election.[64] He explains the mission and the function of the POTUS Shield:

> POTUS SHIELD is a council of prelates that is assembling to raise up a spiritual shield. You are invited to join us as we bring this anointed assembly in intercession, prayers, declarations, and decrees of The Word of the Lord across our nation! We are gathering as the POTUS SHIELD to prepare the way for the shift in our nation![65]

One of the POTUS Shield's objectives was to engage in spiritual warfare in favor of President Trump. For example, during his [first] impeachment trial, Amedia claimed that the attacks against Trump came from a "spirit of witchcraft" and a "twisted conspiracy" from demonic forces. The POTUS Shield viewed itself as "God's spiritual weapon." Amedia believed that Trump's enemies would be defeated because the Lord is "a man of war."[66] Amedia also frequently applied verses from the Psalms to President Trump: "I pursued my enemies and overtook them; I did not turn back till they were destroyed ... you humbled my adversaries before me." (Ps. 18.37–39).[67]

Likewise, for Wallnau, Trump's enemies, particularly the mainstream media, are under the influence of evil powers. During another interview on the *Jim Bakker Show*, Wallnau discussed how the media's opposition to Trump is demonic in nature: "I'll tell you what's happening: Isaiah 45. If you want to know how to pray for the president, remember it's Leviathan who is twisting every piece of news in order to dismember people from this man."[68] Like many other Charismatics, Wallnau interprets the Leviathan, a mythical sea monster (see Ps. 74.14; 104.26; Job 3.8; 40.20–41.25; Isa. 27.1), spiritually. He speaks of the "spirit of Leviathan" as an evil principality which twists the truth and leads the people into error concerning Trump.[69] Wallnau invited Christians to join in prayer against this twisted Leviathan spirit which sought, through media influence, to turn the electorate away from the former American president.

The Spirit of Jezebel, Abortion, and Civil War

Abortion has been a key issue of the cultural war led by the Christian right in the United States. Charismatic Trump supporters fight relentlessly seeking to overthrow abortion rights. Michael L. Brown,[70] a pastor, author, apologist, and well-known radio host of Charismatic persuasion, believed that the debate over abortion would lead the nation toward a second civil war[71]:

> A civil war is coming to America, only this time, it will be abortion, rather than slavery, that divides the nation. And while I hope with all my heart that it will not be a physically violent war, the ideological conflict will certainly be violent and intense.[72]

Brown claimed that the ideological conflict was driven by a demonic entity called "Jezebel." In the Bible, Jezebel was the wife of Ahab, King of Israel. She is described as an idolater who successfully used her seductive powers to establish herself in the political sphere. Jezebel ordered the assassination of several people, some of whom were God's own prophets in Israel.[73] In the New Testament, she is also mentioned as a woman suspected of being a false prophetess, practicing idolatry, and indulging in sexual immorality.[74] For Brown, the "spirit of Jezebel" would allegedly still be present today:

> In twenty-first-century America, Jezebel is not a person. But it's as if the spirit of Jezebel is alive again today. The influence of the same demonic force is being felt in the massive increase of pornography and sexual temptation, the militant spirit of abortion, the rise of radical feminism, and most importantly, in the attempt to silence prophetic voices. Just as Jezebel clashed with strong men almost three thousand years ago, the demonic spirit of Jezebel is powerful in America, and it is going after the church.[75]

Brown believes that the societal evils present in America today (pornography, immorality, abortion, radical feminism) are reminiscent of the characteristics of the biblical Jezebel. The opposition to "prophetic voices" is evidently the result of the demonic principality known as "Jezebel." Like White-Cain and Wallnau, Brown also demonizes "flesh and blood" (Eph. 6.12), giving concrete embodiment to the "spirit of Jezebel," notably under the guise of feminist movements. According to Brown, the country must shift direction and revert to its "Judeo-Christian" roots. This is where Donald Trump comes into play. Brown compared the former president to King Jehu, the military commander who was responsible for the death of Jezebel and her husband, King Ahab, as mentioned in 2 Kings 9–10.[76] God used Jehu to deliver Israel from the grip of this idolatrous couple. Brown suggested a surprising point of comparison between Trump and Jehu predicated on the idea that Jehu drove his chariot like a maniac (2 Kings 9.20). Since the mainstream media characterize Trump's conduct as crazy, Brown inferred that, as with Jehu, Trump would destroy the "spirit of Jezebel" which prevailed over the United States. The comparison was analogous to the one offered by Lance Wallnau, who declared Trump to be a divine "wrecking ball," a new Cyrus chosen by God.[77]

Another televangelist, Rick Joyner,[78] also predicted that the current cultural battle would eventually lead to a new civil war in the nation. Joyner claimed that he had a prophetic dream from God about the upcoming conflict, which he saw as imminent:

> On Dec. 14, 2018, I had a dream about various attacks coming upon our country. I was also shown those who would be sent out to counter each one. [...] We are already in the first stages of the Second American Revolutionary/Civil War. [...] As the saying goes, "If we do not change our direction, we will end up where we are headed." We don't have to be a prophet to see that we're headed for civil war. Even so, before the dream I felt that we still had a long way to go before it became "inevitable." In the dream, I saw that we had already crossed that line and it is now upon us, so we must change our strategy from trying to avoid it to winning it. [...] The whole world is entering the most trying times there has ever been. What we will be given to face them is a sure hope from above that the outcome will be "successful."[79]

According to Joyner, the United States had reached a point of no return, the line having already been crossed. Believers could no longer hope to avoid the conflict; they now had to ensure victory. Joyner and Trump's Charismatic supporters believed that the former president's involvement was necessary to win the cultural conflict.

Many evangelicals favorable toward the former president hastened to suggest that a civil war could occur if Trump were to lose his power. Franklin Graham declared: "If the president was brought down for whatever reason, it could lead to a civil war. There are millions of people out there that voted for President Trump that are behind him that are angry and they are mad."[80] Robert Jeffress, senior pastor of the First Baptist Church of Dallas,[81] had a similar reaction during an interview on *Fox News*: if the Democrats succeeded at stripping the president of his office, this would cause a profound fracture, a civil war which would forever damage the nation.[82] Jeffress' reply pleased Trump, who promptly shared the pastor's comments on his own Twitter account.[83] Frequent proponents of conspiracy theories among evangelicals tended to express the same concerns. Pastor Rick Wiles[84] put it this way:

> If you try to take Donald Trump out of the White House [...] you're going to push mild, law-abiding, middle-class Americans to pick up their

firearms and defend the Republic against seditious traitors and radicals because the Democratic Party is now the Communist Party of the United States of America.[85]

Wiles not only stigmatized Democrats as communists but also claimed that Trump's impeachment would incite voters to resort to violence to defend their rights.

Americans who opposed the president's impeachment found the references to violence to be relatable. *The Hill*, a website that provides nonpartisan information about life in and behind the scenes of Congress, reported on comments made by Trump supporters during a rally in November 2019, stating that the president's removal *"would cause physical violence in this country that we haven't seen since the first Civil War. I think it would become the second Civil War,"* [...] *"There'll be a lot of mad Americans. Possibly, 70, 80 thousand—70, 80 million Americans on the loose, not very happy. What we're seeing is a divided country. Both sides are dug in, no one's budging."*[86] For many Christians who voted for this president, the cultural war could not be won if he were no longer in power. A significant part of the former president's support hinged on "biblical" justifications: Trump was understood to be a new Cyrus or a contemporary Jehu about to undo the "spirit of Jezebel." As we will now see, Trump's 2020 re-election campaign was also viewed through the lens of spiritual warfare.

Trump's Re-Election Campaign and "The Political Spirit"

In May 2019, Lance Wallnau was once again invited on the *Jim Bakker Show* to set the stage for Trump's re-election in 2020. On the show, Wallnau said that Christians should take control of the "spiritual atmosphere" in the United States, because there would be a heightened civil war sentiment during the upcoming presidential election:

> It will be like when Lincoln was elected in the Civil War. [...] As believers we actually have to take ownership of the spiritual atmosphere over America and instead of worrying about the future, we've got to recognize we have authority in the spirit realm. We have to start using it. I'm convinced that there's underutilized potential in the body of Christ that's got to come to the surface within the next 16 months. [...] The Democratic Party—and we need to know this—has been taken over. [...] But now, ideologically, the left has a movement within it that has got *into* the Democratic Party to seize power. So, what you've got is the radical new element that is taking over the party and *pulling* it in their direction. That's where the socialism comes from.[87]

In this brief excerpt, Wallnau raised the specter of civil war and emphasized the importance for Christians—who make up the body of Christ—to reclaim their authority in the spirit realm. Once again, the language is that of spiritual warfare. The reference to the "spiritual atmosphere" is an allusion to Ephesians 6.12. Wallnau relied on his listeners to make the connection with the battle against evil spirits in heavenly places. He urged Christians to take action against the demonic forces which allegedly have a hold on the United States. Then, once again, the prophet shifted his focus from the spiritual realm to Trump's political adversaries, namely, the Democratic Party. According to Wallnau, the Democratic Party has been infiltrated by "the left" and would implement socialism if elected. Voting for Democrats means supporting socialism. Many people in the United States view socialism as the opposite of American capitalism and often associate it with communism.[88] Republicans brandish the fear of socialism to undermine the values of liberty, rights, and prosperity that are dear to many Americans. Labeling political opponents as "socialists" implies that they are unfit to lead the country. In order to take control of the spiritual atmosphere in the United States, Wallnau believed that political adversaries must be neutralized, and engaging in political activities against the Democratic Party is seen as a way for Christians to exercise their authority. Wallnau seemed to think that defeating evil principalities in heavenly places would result in a Democratic Party debacle in the 2020 elections.

But a Democratic victory could also lead to deadly violence against Christian leaders, according to Jim Bakker. Bakker reasoned that some people never accepted Trump's 2016 victory and still question how he had been elected at the head of the country:

> Because God's people voted and the world knows it, the enemies of the Gospel know it. I'm going to say something I probably shouldn't say. What's coming next, if we keep losing, you're going to see the leaders of the church and the leaders of the Gospel and the political conservative leaders that are powerful, you are going to see them suddenly die, suddenly killed—suddenly as they were driving, suddenly as they were in a boat, suddenly in an airplane—you're going to see it one after another. God spoke this to me years ago what would happen near the end, and I believe we're in that time. This is life and death. This is—the hatred of murder is in the country.[89]

"The leaders of the church and the leaders of the Gospel" is an unconventional expression. It may refer to non-denominational Christian leaders, such as the types of ministries discussed in Chapter 2. It is also interesting that the "leaders of the church and the leaders of the Gospel" are on equal footing with the "political leaders that are powerful." Bakker was clearly capitalizing on people's fear that a Trump defeat would give free reign to the enemies of Christians. Conservative politicians and evangelical decision-makers would suddenly be in mortal danger due to their faith and support for the president. This end times conspiratorial scenario to play out in America was allegedly imparted to Bakker by means of a revelation from God. Trump's political opponents were once again demonized. Charismatic leaders fuel their own persecution complex with secular society through such revelations. Convinced that attempts are being made to silence them, they often fall into conspiratorial thinking.

Kris Vallotton, one of the senior leaders of Bethel Church in Redding, California, shared a similar view. He claimed that a "political spirit," a demonic entity, divided Christians and sought to silence their voice and do them harm during the 2020 election.[90] The role of this "political spirit," according to Vallotton, was to create division by highlighting the past misdeeds of the candidates, thereby sowing confusion about the presidential election. The logic is once again that of spiritual warfare. Vallotton had already spoken about the presence of a "political spirit" during the 2016 elections[91] and acknowledged that the candidate he supported was not flawless—a position akin to that of C. Peter Wagner mentioned in Chapter 2.

This warning against the divisive effects of the "political spirit" came a few weeks after Mark Galli, former editor-in-chief of *Christianity Today*,[92] called for Trump's removal from office.[93] *Christianity Today*, founded by Billy Graham in 1956, has a monthly readership of 4.5 million and is considered by the mainstream media to be "evangelicalism's flagship magazine."[94]

In his editorial, Galli claimed that the president's immoral conduct was an attack on the integrity of all evangelicals in the United States. Although the former president was not impeached by the Senate, Galli's editorial clearly sent shock waves throughout the evangelical world. Indeed, Trump's evangelical supporters, led primarily by the movement's Charismatic wing, reacted sharply to Galli's remarks. A letter containing 200 signatures was published in support of the former president. The letter stated that Galli's editorial was detrimental and challenged "the spiritual integrity and Christian witness of tens-of-millions of believers who take seriously their civic and moral obligations"[95] in voting for Trump. The clash between these two groups within American evangelicalism has led to a strong mobilization of "Evangelicals for Trump."[96] After the controversial editorial in *Christianity Today*, Steven Strang, founder of *Charisma Magazine*,[97] characterized Trump's presidency in terms of spiritual warfare. If he were not re-elected in November 2020, it could negatively impact believers in the United States.[98]

Notes

1 In the days immediately after its posting, the video of this "warfare prayer" was viewed more than 2 million times.

2 https://twitter.com/RightWingWatch/status/1220740601781608448/ (accessed 26 May 2023).

3 https://twitter.com/JamesMartinSJ/status/1221436968502022149/ (accessed 26 May 2023).

4 https://twitter.com/DrJenGunter/status/1221248958443524096/ (accessed 26 May 2023).

5 https://twitter.com/costiwhinn/status/1221265664830164993/ (accessed 21 March 2020).

6 https://twitter.com/ChurchofSatan/status/1221278603809214465/ (accessed 26 May 2023).

7 For example, see https://twitter.com/seankent/status/1221281967603363846/ as well as https://twitter.com/rabiasquared/status/1221277141775589376/ (accessed 26 May 2023).

8 https://twitter.com/Paula_White/status/1221456959368507392/ (accessed 26 May 2023).

9 https://voiceofthelight.com/about-us/ana-mendez-ferrell/ (accessed 26 May 2023).

10 See her promotional video of one such expedition: https://youtu.be/v2WGqX6NR3Y/ (accessed 22 March 2020).

11 Daniel K. Olukoya is a Nigerian minister and founder of Mountain of Fire and Miracles Ministries, a global association of Pentecostal churches which has been in existence since 1989; see https://www.mountainoffire.org/ (accessed 26 May 2023). On prayer and the political praxis of spiritual warfare, see Adelakun (2023).

12 Deceased in 2019, Pat Holliday was a pastor and founder of Miracle Internet Church in Florida; see https://www.miracleinternetchurch.com/ (accessed 26 May 2023).

13 Jennifer LeClaire is a senior leader of Awakening House of Prayer in Fort Lauderdale, Florida. She is also the founder of the network *Ignite* and of the prayer movement *Awakening Prayer Hubs*; see https://jenniferleclaire.org/ (accessed 26 May 2023).

14 Olukoya (2012); Holliday (2013a and 2013b); LeClaire (2018).

15 See her teaching on this subject during a prophetic conference: https://youtu.be/mcapLBXx4j0/ (accessed 26 May 2023).

16 Blog dedicated to speculations concerning the end times and to teachings on spiritual warfare. See https://endtimeswatcher.wordpress.com/2015/03/21/demonic-marine-kingdom/ (accessed 26 May 2023).

17 The marine or water spirit is also a reference to Maame Wata in neo-Pentecostal African circles. Maame Wata is a mermaid/ marine spirit portrayed as having a female upper body with the tail of a fish. She is often called the Queen of the Coast and sometimes referred to as the spirit of Jezebel; see, Asamoah-Gyadu (2005, pp. 171–2).

18 Jennifer Eivaz is the executive pastor of Harvest Church in Turlock, California, and hosts the podcast *Take Ten with Jenn*; see https://www.jennifereivaz.com/ (accessed 26 May 2023).

19 See article by Marti Pieper, "The Leviathan Spirit and the Crocodile Have This Dangerous Characteristic in Common": https://www.charismamag.com/life/women/44483-the-leviathan-spirit-and-the-crocodile-have-this-dangerous-characteristic-in-common/ (accessed 22 March 2020).

20 Eckhardt (2014, pp. 185–6).

21 Olukoya (2010).

22 See Gonzalez for a detailed analysis of the event and of White-Cain's prayer (2019, pp. 152–4).

23 See https://www.youtube.com/watch?v=MY4MYPCzAfk/ (accessed 26 May 2023).

24 The "horn" is an image representing power and strength (see Mic. 4.13 and Zech. 1.21).

25 See https://www.youtube.com/watch?v=MY4MYPCzAfk/ (accessed 26 May 2023).

26 "He reveals deep and hidden things; he knows what lies in darkness, and light dwells with him." (Dan. 2.22).

27 For the Trump administration and its supporters, the "Deep State" is part of the government system which interferes with their political functioning. This applies to all political actors and jurisdictions—whether Democratic or Republican—which prevent Trump from doing his work; see https://www.businessinsider.com/what-deep-state-is-and-why-trump-gets-it-wrong-2020-1/ (accessed 26 May 2023).

28 The Mueller investigation aimed at determining if there was collusion between Russia and Trump's campaign team during the 2016 election.

29 See the excellent article by Gonzalez on the conspiratorial view of some Charismatics concerning the "Deep State" and the Mueller investigation (2019, pp. 148–52).

30 See https://www.youtube.com/watch?v=MY4MYPCzAfk/ (accessed 26 May 2023).

31 Concerning the warfare prayer, see Gonzalez (2014, pp. 187–223), McAlister (2016).

32 Gonzalez (2008, pp. 46–7) notes that, in the reports of contemporary evangelical missionaries, the devil is characterized as the "enemy," an idea borrowed from the New Testament (see Matt. 13.39; Luke 10.19).

33 The phrasing "in the name of Jesus" is inspired by this saying attributed to Jesus in the Gospel according to John: "And I will do whatever you ask in my name, so that the Father may be glorified in the Son. You may ask me for anything in my name, and I will do it." (John 14.13–14). See Gonzalez (2013, pp. 82–3; 2014, p. 250) concerning the authority and power that Charismatics attribute to the words "in the name of Jesus."

34 See Wagner (1992, pp. 16–9).

35 For a summary of the three levels proposed by Wagner, see https://adioma.com/@ChristianRightXposed/infographic/three-levels-of-spiritual-warfare/ (accessed 26 May 2023).

36 Those who claim to have a "deliverance ministry" hold the power to deliver people from the grip of demons, in sum, an exorcism power. This sort of activity was popularized among evangelicals by authors such as Anderson (2000) and Murphy (2003).

37 On the question of territories under demonic control, see Fer (2007) and McAlister (2014).

38 Wagner (2012, p. 78).

39 Wagner (1996, p. 89).

40 Note that the text from Deuteronomy is that of the Septuagint (LXX), the Greek version of the Old Testament.

41 The end differs in the Hebrew text: "… after the children of Israel." It is important to mention that the Greek version contains, in this case, the oldest form of the biblical text.

42 Frederick Fyvie Bruce (1910–1990) was a professor of biblical studies at the University of Manchester in England and was one of the most influential evangelical exegetes of the 20th century.

43 See Wagner (2012, p. 79) and White (2012, pp. 84–5).

44 See also Dan. 8.21; 11.2; Zech. 9.13.

45 Wagner (2012, p. 80).

46 Wagner (1992, pp. 89–94).

47 For other New Testament examples, see Wagner (1996).

48 Peretti is a Canadian evangelical author of Christian fiction focused primarily on the supernatural world. *This Present Darkness* was published in 1986 and *Piercing the Darkness* in 1989.

49 See Gonzalez (2014, pp. 256–7).

50 George Otis, Jr., is the founder and president of The Sentinel Group, an agency for media research and Christian training located in Seattle, helping communities eager for renewal to engage in social transformation; see also: https://www. sentinelgroup.org/ (accessed 26 May 2023).

51 Otis, Jr. (1991, pp. 85–6) and Holvast (2009).

52 The Joshua Project "is a research initiative seeking to highlight the ethnic people groups of the world with the fewest followers of Christ"; see https:// joshuaproject.net/resources/articles/10_40_window (accessed 26 May 2023).

53 See Otis, Jr. (1999, pp. 227–42).

54 Otis, Jr. (1999, p. 253).

55 Wagner documented two long—and very strange— "prayer walking" expeditions to battle "the Queen of Heaven," an evil principality who allegedly occupies the top of Mount Everest. According to Wagner, this evil principality was also the manifestation of the Greek goddess Diana, who once sat in the temple of the city of Ephesus; see Wagner (2000b and 2001).

56 See Gonzalez's detailed analysis concerning the significance of "demonic networks" and the reaction of the media and of some evangelicals to White-Cain's prayer (2019, pp. 148–61).

57 See https://www.youtube.com/watch?v=MY4MYPCzAfk/ (accessed 26 May 2023).

58 Concerning the exercise of "apostolic" decrees of justice, see http://www. elijahlist.com/words/display_word.html?ID=2558/ (accessed 16 March 2020).

59 https://www.youtube.com/watch?v=0XhVtSRR7aI/ (accessed 26 May 2023).

60 https://twitter.com/lancewallnau/status/1226572609946558467/ (accessed 26 May 2023).

61 https://www.youtube.com/watch?v=qQbGnJd9poc&NR=1/ (accessed 26 May 2023).

62 POTUS is the acronym for President Of The United States. Read Peter Montgomery, "POTUS Shield: Trump's Dominionist Prayer Warriors and the 'Prophetic Order of the United States'": https://www.rightwingwatch.org/report/ potus-shield-trumps-dominionist-prayer-warriors-and-the-prophetic-order-of-the-united-states/ (accessed 26 May 2023).

63 See https://www.touchheaven.com/pastor-frank-and-lorilee-amedia/ (accessed 26 May 2023).

64 See https://jimbakkershow.com/guest-bios/frank-lorilee-amedia/ (accessed 26 May 2023).

65 https://www.potusshield.com/ (accessed 26 May 2023).

66 This expression is taken from Exodus 15.3: "The Lord is a warrior."

67 Peter Montgomery, "POTUS Shield: 'God is a Man of War' Who Will 'Bring Disaster' on Trump's Opponents": https://www.rightwingwatch.org/post/potus-shield-god-is-a-man-of-war-who-will-bring-disaster-on-trumps-opponents/ (accessed 26 May 2023).

68 See https://www.youtube.com/watch?v=vkn7yMRrbWM/ (accessed 26 May 2023).

69 To understand the significance which Wallnau and White-Cain give what they call the "twisted spirit" of Leviathan, see their discussion on the subject: https:// subsplash.com/paulawhiteministries/lb/mi/+cntz4p9/ (accessed 26 May 2023).

70 Michael L. Brown is also the founder of FIRE School of Ministry in Concord, North Carolina; see https://askdrbrown.org/biography/ (accessed 26 May 2023).

71 See Jason Wilson, "Christian Rightwingers Warn Abortion Fight Could Spark US Civil War": https://www.theguardian.com/world/2019/may/26/abortion-ban-rightwing-christian-figures-civil-war-predictions/ (accessed 26 May 2023).

72 Michael L. Brown, "The coming civil war over abortion": https://www.christianpost.com/voices/the-coming-civil-war-over-abortion.html/ (accessed 26 May 2023).

73 See 1 Kings 16.30–32; 19.2; 21.5–29; 2 Kings 9.22, 30–7.

74 Rev. 2.20-23.

75 From the cover of his latest book, *Jezebel's War with America: The Plot to Destroy Our Country and What You Can Do to Defeat It.*

76 See https://www.youtube.com/watch?v=F1HVzsTzGPA&feature=emb_logo/ (accessed 26 May 2023).

77 See Chapter 1.

78 Rick Joyner is the founder and director general of MorningStar Ministries and Heritage International Ministries, as well as president of the interdenominational movement The OAK Initiative. In addition, Joyner is the senior pastor of MorningStar Fellowship Church in Fort Mill, South Carolina; see https://morningstarfortmill.com/ (accessed 26 May 2023).

79 Rick Joyner, "We Are in First Stages of America's Second Revolutionary War": https://charismamag.com/blogs/propheticfire/rick-joyner-we-are-in-first-stages-of-america-s-second-revolutionary-war/ (accessed 27 May 2023).

80 See Samuel Smith, "Franklin Graham: Trump's enemies will hurt America, could spark civil war if impeached": https://www.christianpost.com/news/franklin-graham-trumps-enemies-will-hurt-america-could-spark-civil-war-if-impeached.html?page=2/ (accessed 26 May 2023).

81 https://www.firstdallas.org/ (accessed 26 May 2023).

82 https://www.mediamatters.org/robert-jeffress/fox-news-contributor-robert-jeffress-if-trump-successfully-impeached-it-will-cause (accessed 26 May 2023).

83 See https://twitter.com/realDonaldTrump/status/1178477539653771264/ (accessed 26 May 2023).

84 Rick Wiles is an American conspiracist and senior pastor of Flowing Streams Church in Vero Beach, Florida. He is also the founder of *TruNews*, an alternative information network promoting racist and anti-Semitic conspiracy theories.

85 https://twitter.com/RightWingWatch/status/1179051248672227333/ (accessed 26 May 2023).

86 See Aris Folley, "Trump supporter says his removal could lead to the 'second Civil War'": https://thehill.com/blogs/blog-briefing-room/news/474192-trump-supporter-says-his-removal-could-lead-to-the-second-civil/ (accessed 26 May 2023).

87 https://youtu.be/c2i4B4T96RU/ (accessed 26 May 2023).

88 On this question, see Hofstadter (1964), Heffer (1988), and Heale (1990).

89 See Kyle Mantyla, "Jim Bakker: Christian Leaders and Politicians Will Be Murdered if Trump is not Re-Elected": https://www.rightwingwatch.org/post/jim-bakker-christian-leaders-and-politicians-will-be-murdered-if-trump-is-not-re-elected/ (accessed 26 May 2023).

90 Kris Vallotton, "Bethel Pastor: American Church, It's Time to Speak Up!": https://www.charismanews.com/opinion/80161-bethel-pastor-american-church-it-s-time-to-speak-up/ (accessed 26 May 2023).

91 See https://www.krisvallotton.com/ugly-election-with-a-pretty-face/ (accessed 26 May 2023).

92 See https://www.christianitytoday.org/ (accessed 26 May 2023).

93 Mark Galli, "Trump Should Be Removed From Office": https://www.christianitytoday.com/ct/2019/december-web-only/trump-should-be-removed-from-office.html/ (accessed 26 May 2023).

94 See https://www.washingtonpost.com/national/religion/why-a-yes-to-gays-is-often-a-no-to-evangelicalism-commentary/2015/06/10/d8657e06-0fa6-11e5-a0fe-dccfea4653ee_story.html (accessed 26 May 2023).

95 Melissa Barnhart, "Nearly 200 Evangelical Leaders Slam Christianity Today for Questioning Their Christian Witness": https://www.christianpost.com/news/nearly-200-evangelical-leaders-slam-christianity-today-for-questioning-their-christian-witness.html/ (accessed 26 May 2023). Mark Galli resigned from *Christianity Today* in January 2020.

96 As previously mentioned, a meeting of "Evangelicals for Trump" took place in Miami, on January 3, 2020.

97 In addition to being the founder of the magazine *Charisma* (Christian magazine produced in Lake Mary, Florida, with content geared toward both Pentecostals and Charismatics) and the CEO of *Charisma Media*, Stephen Strang is also a journalist, author, and entrepreneur. In 2005, Strang was named among the 25 most influential evangelical personalities in America by *Time* magazine; see http://content.time.com/time/specials/packages/article/0,28804,1993235_1993243_1993319,00.html (accessed 26 May 2023).

98 Stephen Strang, "Why We Can't Afford to Ignore Our Nation's Spiritual Warfare Any Longer": https://www.charismanews.com/opinion/79512-why-we-can-t-afford-to-ignore-our-nation-s-spiritual-warfare-any-longer/ (accessed 26 May 2023).

4

WHEN IS THE END OF THE WORLD? ESCHATOLOGICAL FICTIONS AND THEIR POLITICAL CONSEQUENCES

On January 3, 2020, President Trump authorized a drone strike that killed Iranian General Qassem Soleimani at Baghdad International Airport.[1] The news caused a stir in Iran[2] and around the world, as well as among some evangelicals in the United States. Many of these Christians saw this event as a clear indication of the "end times" and a precursor to the second coming of Christ. These believers use current events to decipher the "signs of the times," interpreting them through the lens of certain "biblical prophecies" believed to foretell the end of the world.

Many evangelicals in the United States are devoted to studying "eschatology," i.e., doctrines concerning the end of the world. They have differing views, however, on the timeline of events, specifically on how and when Jesus will return. Some Charismatic Trump supporters may have a more flexible approach to eschatology, as they strive to establish God's Kingdom while anticipating Christ's return.

A significant number of evangelicals view eschatology through a geo-political lens. Many supported Trump's decision to recognize the city of Jerusalem as the capital of Israel[3] and to move the American embassy from Tel Aviv to Jerusalem on May 14, 2018.[4] A survey by LifeWay Research in 2017[5] found that 80% of evangelicals believed that the birth of the modern State of Israel in 1948 and the return of the Jews to their homeland were the fulfillment of "biblical prophecies" that pointed to Christ's second coming.[6] They hold to the idea that in the "last days" Jews will convert to Christianity and recognize Jesus as their Messiah. According to their interpretation of biblical texts, Jerusalem should be recognized as the sole capital of the modern State of Israel. The city is the preeminent place of the God's presence, and the Bible presents it as eternal and indivisible. Many believers close

DOI: 10.4324/9781003358718-5

to American power claim that Jews are God's people, and the city must be exclusively under Jewish control, as it was in the time of King David.[7] This view excludes Palestinians from the divine plan.

This recognition of the Hebrew State is part of a strategy aimed at rebuilding the Temple in Jerusalem.[8] The Temple Institute, an educational and religious organization founded by the Rabbi Yisrael Ariel in 1987[9] and located in the Jewish Quarter of the Old City, has the objective "to see Israel rebuild the Holy Temple on Mount Moriah in Jerusalem, in accord with the biblical commandments."[10] Some popular evangelical interpretations of biblical prophecy suggest that the reconstruction of the Temple will be made possible by the rise of an Antichrist figure, who will make a seven-year covenant with the Jewish people.[11] This world leader will rise to power in the last days. He will promote world peace and establish a world government, but as the Antichrist, he will also set up a false religion and persecute those who do not recognize him as the Messiah. We will return to this topic shortly.

It is therefore not surprising that some people in positions of power, such as former American Secretary of State Mike Pompeo, are influenced by eschatological ideas. Pompeo spoke in 2015 about waiting for the rapture of the Church*,[12] when Christ returns to take believers (both living and dead) to heaven with him. Some Christians interpreted the death of Iranian General Soleimani as a sign that the "rapture" is approaching and that we are entering the last days before Christ's second coming.

To better understand the impact of these concepts on American politics, it is crucial to recognize the various interpretive paradigms concerning biblical prophecies. In the following section, we will examine the different eschatological models used by some Charismatic leaders to interpret political events as indications of the "end times."

Paradigms of Biblical Prophecy

Within the evangelical world, there are different ways to interpret biblical prophecies. The term "prophecy" can carry several meanings, such as the proclamation of God's word to his people, without any predictions about the future. In antiquity, prophets addressed their contemporaries, and their messages were meant for that time. Today, however, people interested in eschatology also believe that biblical prophecy foretells the future. They argue that certain events mentioned in books such as Revelation, Daniel, Ezekiel, or Zechariah have not happened yet. In a general sense, evangelicals typically interpret biblical prophecies using one of four different hermeneutic paradigms.[13]

According to the "preterist" paradigm,[14] prophetic writings were about events which had already taken place. The book of Revelation, for example, was not about the end times, but addressed the biblical author's contemporaries.

Likewise, Jesus' eschatological discourse in Chapter 24 of Matthew's Gospel is understood as referring to the First Jewish Revolt, which ended in the destruction of Jerusalem and the Temple (66–70 CE). In this perspective, biblical authors were writing to 1st-century Christians who were struggling under the tyranny of the Roman Empire.

"Partial" preterism is an intermediate position which holds that certain biblical prophecies have been fulfilled while others have not. Certain passages in the book of Revelation or the Gospel of Matthew, for example, allude to past events, yet other prophecies contained in these books will only be fulfilled in the last days.

The "idealist" paradigm interprets prophetic and apocalyptic texts symbolically. The book of Revelation is notably replete with visions, colors, numbers, and exotic beasts, many of which simply represent the conflict between good and evil. These symbols have no historical significance.

Biblical prophecies, according to the "futurist" paradigm, predicted events involving the end of the world. In this view, most of the content found in the book of Revelation and in Matthew 24 describes events yet to come. Many evangelicals share this perspective. For example, this paradigm informed the way a number of evangelicals in the United States interpreted the assassination of Soleimani as a sign of the end times.

The Charismatic leaders who supported Trump tend to oscillate between two approaches, either a "partial" preterist interpretation or a "futurist" understanding. And, in fact, these two interpretive paradigms undergird three types of eschatologies—doctrinal speculations about the end times—which today have significant geopolitical consequences due to the political influence of American evangelicals.

Some Eschatological Ideas

Dispensationalism

The death of Soleimani elicited a strong reaction from evangelicals who adhere to "premillennial" dispensationalism. We will elaborate further on two complex concepts crucial for our understanding of the eschatological worldview shared by many evangelicals.

We begin with dispensationalism. This theological system was popularized in the 19th century by John Nelson Darby,[15] an Anglo-Irish evangelist associated with the Plymouth Brethren.[16] According to this theological framework, biblical history consists of different "dispensations" or means to salvation.[17] Dispensationalism serves both as a way of interpreting the Bible and as a theology of history. One of the peculiarities of this theological system is how it explains God's interactions with the nation of Israel and the Church*, which are seen as two distinct groups each with their own destiny. According to this system, the time of the Church*—called the dispensation of grace—was unknown to the prophets of the Old Testament and is a sort of parenthesis in God's plan for the ages. The two final "dispensations," grace and the millennial reign, are especially significant for those interested in eschatology.

The "Rapture of the Church*"

Dispensationalism centers on the idea of the "rapture" of Christ's Church* to heaven. It is important to differentiate between the second coming of Christ and the rapture of the Church*. According to dispensationalist interpretation, the "rapture" is a biblical concept, found in 1 Thessalonians 4.15–17:

> 4[15] According to the Lord's word, we tell you that we who are still alive, who are left until the coming of the Lord, will certainly not precede those who have fallen asleep.[16] For the Lord himself will come down from heaven, with a loud command, with the voice of the archangel and with the trumpet call of God, and the dead in Christ will rise first.[17] After that, we who are still alive and are left will be caught up together with them in the clouds to meet the Lord in the air. And so, we will be with the Lord forever.

Before his triumphal return, Christ will *secretly* return on the clouds to rapture his Church*. The dead "in Christ," which refers to true believers who will have died prior to the rapture, will be resurrected, and the living Christians who experience the event will be transformed and clothed in glorious bodies, as if they also underwent the resurrection.[18] These two groups will then be raptured to heaven to live with God.

This event will be the trigger for the rest of the dispensational end-time scenario. Following the rapture, there will be the "seven-year tribulation," during which God's judgments will rain down on those remaining on earth—those that have been "left behind"—culminating with the battle of Armageddon, the last planetary conflict when all the nations will assemble in Israel to make war on the Jewish people. Only after the "seven-year tribulation" will Christ's *visible* second coming take place, where he will *visibly* return with the Church*—the believers who were removed from the earth during the rapture—to battle the forces of the Antichrist and the enemies of Israel, and to establish his thousand-year reign on earth.[19]

The "Seven-Year Tribulation"

Part of the dispensational eschatological framework rests on a particular interpretation of Daniel 9.24–27, which focuses on a period of "70 weeks," pertaining to the history of the Jewish people.[20] The revelation solely concerns Israel and not Christians.

9^{24} Seventy 'sevens' are decreed for your people and your holy city to finish transgression, to put an end to sin, to atone for wickedness, to bring in everlasting righteousness, to seal up vision and prophecy and to anoint the Most Holy Place.^{25} Know and understand this: From the time the word goes out to restore and rebuild Jerusalem until the Anointed One, the ruler, comes, there will be seven 'sevens,' and sixty-two 'sevens.' It will be rebuilt with streets and a trench, but in times of trouble.^{26} After the sixty-two 'sevens,' the Anointed One will be put to death and will have nothing. The people of the ruler who will come will destroy the city and the sanctuary. The end will come like a flood: War will continue until the end, and desolations have been decreed.^{27} He will confirm a covenant with many for one 'seven.' In the middle of the 'seven' he will put an end to sacrifice and offering. And at the temple he will set up an abomination that causes desolation, until the end that is decreed is poured out on him.

This period of "70 weeks" is interpreted as "seventy-seven," with "seven" being a unit of time, such as seven days, hours, months, years, etc. However, many eschatological enthusiasts of dispensational persuasion believe that the units refer to years. "Seventy" would be units of "seven years." Multiplying "seventy units" of "seven years" by seven (70 x 7) equals 490 years. Daniel's "70 weeks" would therefore correspond to 490 years.

This dispensational reading suggests that the 70 weeks—or the 490 years—begin with the announcement to rebuild the city of Jerusalem, which occurred either in 458 BCE or 444 BCE.^{21} A time frame is calculated as "seven weeks" (= 49 years) plus "sixty-two weeks" (= 434 years) for a total of 69 weeks (= 483 years). When added to the year of the decree of Jerusalem's reconstruction, the calculation brings us to the approximate date of Jesus' crucifixion.^{22} The entire dispensational system rests on the idea that Daniel's 70 weeks represent a precise chronological time frame of 490 years.

Dispensationalists believe there is a long hiatus between Daniel's 69th and 70th weeks and identify two events which happened during that time. First, "the Anointed One will be put to death" (Daniel 9.26), which they believe to be a reference to the crucifixion of Jesus. Second, "the people of the ruler who will come will destroy the city and the sanctuary" (Daniel 9.26), which is interpreted as the destruction of Jerusalem and its Temple in the year 70 CE. Now only one week remains, the "70th week" (Dan. 9.27) which is still to come. This final remaining week, according to their calculations, will follow the rapture of the Church*. They interpret Daniel's 70th week to be the notorious "seven-year tribulation."

Daniel 9.26–27 mentions the rise of a "ruler," who will make a covenant "with many" during one "seven"—that is "seven years." According to the dispensational reading of Daniel 9.27, the "ruler" is the Antichrist, the end-times political leader, who will make a covenant with the Jewish people to

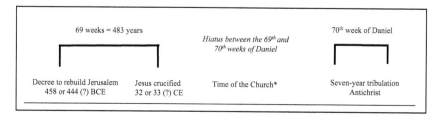

FIGURE 4.1 Dispensational Interpretation of Daniel's 70 Weeks (Dan. 9.24-27).

rebuild their Temple in Jerusalem and reinstate their rituals and sacrifices. However, Daniel 9.27 also reads that "in the middle of the week,"[23] the "ruler" will break his covenant and desecrate the Temple, leading to the persecution of the Jewish people.[24] Afterwards, the Antichrist will be destroyed at the *visible* return of Christ, to occur at the end of the 70th week (Dan. 9.27; 2 Thess. 2.8) (Figure 4.1).

The dispensational system relies on the hypothesis of a hiatus between Daniel's 69th and 70th weeks when the Messiah's crucifixion and the destruction of Jerusalem would have occurred. It is believed that the events associated with Daniel's final week, the 70th week (Daniel 9.27), have not yet come to pass. This final week is what dispensationalists view as the "seven-year tribulation." It will be followed by Christ's *visible* return to establish his millennial reign.

The Millennial Reign

The "millennium" or the "millennial reign" is a thousand-year period, an idea taken from Revelation 20.1–6:

> 20[1] And I saw an angel coming down out of heaven, having the key to the Abyss and holding in his hand a great chain.[2] He seized the dragon, that ancient serpent, who is the devil, or Satan, and bound him for a thousand years.[3] He threw him into the Abyss, and locked and sealed it over him, to keep him from deceiving the nations anymore until the thousand years were ended. After that, he must be set free for a short time.[4] I saw thrones on which were seated those who had been given authority to judge. And I saw the souls of those who had been beheaded because of their testimony about Jesus and because of the word of God. They had not worshipped the beast or its image and had not received its mark on their foreheads or their hands. They came to life and reigned with Christ a thousand years.[5] (The rest of the dead did not come to life until the thousand years were ended.) This is the first resurrection.[6] Blessed and holy are those who share in the first resurrection. The second death has no power over them, but they will be priests of God and of Christ and will reign with him for a thousand years.

We will focus on the commonly accepted views of the millennium, especially those which align with the political ambitions of the Charismatic leaders who supported Trump. "Historic premillennialism" sets the visible return of Christ prior to his millennial reign, following a time of great apostasy (the rejection of faith) and tribulations. The millennium is understood as a literal 1000-year historical period.

Dispensationalism is a theological framework which emphasizes the rapture of the Church* and a seven-year tribulation. It is a form of premillennialism since the rapture of the Church* will occur *before* the millennium. This is always a premillennial perspective. According to dispensationalism, Christ will establish his terrestrial Kingdom in Jerusalem during his millennial reign, after his return to earth. A war called Armageddon will take place just prior to the start of the millennium. We will return to this idea shortly.

For those who view things from a "postmillennial" perspective,[25] the millennium is not understood to be a literal timeframe. Instead, it represents an unspecified period of time where Christ will rule over the earth, but not physically from an earthly throne. He will rule through the spread of the gospel message and through social transformation. Christ's return will occur after the entire world has been gradually Christianized. This theological view is opposite to dispensationalism. The postmillennial perspective is preterist or "partial" preterist, where most of the biblical prophetic texts refer to events which have already occurred. Consequently, there will not be a "seven-year tribulation," nor an "end times" political figure called the Antichrist. In the Bible, the Antichrist or the antichrists was a label given to 1st-century Christians who had fallen away from the faith, denying that Christ was the incarnate Son of God (see 1 John 2.18–22; 4.1–3; 2 John 7). The "Beast" mentioned in Revelation 13 is not a reference to a future Antichrist; rather, it speaks of emperor Nero in the 1st century CE, etc.

In the postmillennial view there is no rapture of the Church* followed by a "seven-year tribulation" in the dispensational sense. If Christians are to be "raptured," it will not occur during a *secret* return of Christ on the clouds; rather, it will happen during his *visible* return across the heavens. Jesus will return to earth with his followers to rule over the entire world after eliminating all evil. But the postmillennial understanding of Jesus' reign is not that of dispensationalists. Rather, the millennium is an ongoing lengthy period that began at Christ's resurrection and ascension. From this time on, Jesus exercises authority over all things and is seated at the right hand of God. The millennium is manifested throughout the history of the Church*, which proclaims and builds God's Kingdom on earth now. Those who embrace the postmillennial perspective expect Jesus to return *after* the millennium to take possession of the Kingdom.

Popularity of the "Rapture of the Church*"

Belief in the rapture is still quite common today. It grew in popularity following the creation of the modern State of Israel in 1948 and the Arab Israeli Six-Day War in 1967. The bestselling book *The Late Great Planet Earth*[26] by Hal Lindsey[27] in the 1970s also contributed to the popularity of the rapture. However, the most widespread dissemination of this idea came through the 16-volume *Left Behind* series by Tim LaHaye and Jerry B. Jenkins.[28] Through this series, LaHaye and Jenkins popularized their dispensationalist interpretation and their perspective on the rapture of the Church*.

LaHaye was born in Detroit on April 27, 1926,[29] and earned a bachelor's degree in 1950 from Bob Jones University, known as one of the bastions of ultra-conservative evangelicalism in the United States. He later obtained a Doctor of Ministry from Western Seminary in Portland, Oregon, and a doctorate in literature from Liberty University in Lynchburg, Virginia. LaHaye served as a pastor in Minneapolis and then in El Cajon, California, for over 20 years. In the 1970s and 1980s, he supported various political groups associated with the Christian right in the United States. He also urged leaders of the religious right to ally themselves with George W. Bush during his 2000 presidential campaign and endorsed former Arkansas governor Mike Huckabee for the Republican presidential nomination in 2008. Huckabee, a Baptist pastor from 1980 to 1992, was a prominent figure in the Christian right, and his daughter, Sarah Huckabee Sanders, served as President Trump's press secretary from 2017 to 2019.

In 1992, LaHaye met Jerry B. Jenkins and proposed a project of turning biblical prophecies into suspense novels. Jenkins, an evangelical author who had previously written fictional stories for both children and adults in popular magazines, agreed to collaborate. The collaboration between LaHaye and Jenkins was to become a gold mine. Published between 1995 and 2007, the *Left Behind* series has sold more than 65 million copies and has been translated into a multitude of languages. This series became a literary phenomenon and inspired the creation of various derivative products such as films, audio dramatizations, video games, and clothing. It is widely regarded as the most popular fiction series in the history of Christian publishing.

These novels are fictional stories about the end times. LaHaye and Jenkins use their own dispensational model and eschatological beliefs to shape the plot. At the end of the prequel titled *The Rapture: In the Twinkling of an Eye/Countdown to the Earth's Last Days*,[30] LaHaye explains why the series has been successful and gives readers a key to understanding the ideas behind the project.[31] LaHaye argues that the series is popular because it is based on biblical prophecies about the end of the world and the return of Christ. According to LaHaye, 65% of Americans believe in the return of Jesus as promised in the Bible. He holds that to truly understand the second coming

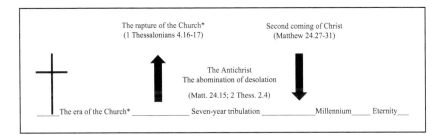

FIGURE 4.2   LaHaye's Dispensational Paradigm.

of Christ, two important reading keys are needed. First, the Bible must be taken literally, including its prophecies. LaHaye points out that confusion arises when biblical prophecies are interpreted as allegories. He disagrees with the postmillennial and preterist readings of Bible prophecy, which he considers to be mistaken. Second, prophecies concerning Christ's return fall into two categories: (1) those which deal with the *secret* rapture of the Church*, and (2) those concerning Christ's *visible* second coming with Christians who had previously been raptured, to establish his millennial reign (Figure 4.2).

LaHaye's note at the end of his prequel is there to ensure that readers clearly understand the eschatological vision depicted in this series. These novels, for LaHaye, are more than just fiction; they contain his dispensational interpretive framework and warn against other eschatological systems which he views as erroneous.

The War of Gog and Magog: A Precursor to the "End Times"

At the end of LaHaye and Jenkins' second prequel, *The Regime: Evil Advances: Before They Were Left Behind*,[32] the State of Israel is attacked by surprise by hundreds of fighter planes. A strange phenomenon occurs, however, and the enemy planes are mysteriously destroyed by fire raining from the sky while the Israeli side suffers no casualties.

For some Charismatic leaders and many other evangelicals, however, this story is not fiction. It depicts what they believe to be an event prophesied in the Bible. In fact, eschatology enthusiasts such as Greg Laurie[33] and Perry Stone argued that the assassination of Iranian General Soleimani and the U.S. stance on Iran could lead to a future coalition of nations, referred in the Bible as "Gog and Magog," that would rise up against the Jewish State.[34]

In fact, one of the characters from LaHaye and Jenkins' prequel explains that the sudden attack on Israel is the fulfillment of a biblical prophecy about the end times. The story is based on a dispensational interpretation of the "Gog and Magog" war, mentioned in the book of the prophet

Ezekiel, specifically Chapters 38 and 39. Here are the most significant sections:

38[2] "Son of man, set your face against Gog, of the land of Magog, the chief prince of Meshek and Tubal; prophesy against him[3] and say: 'This is what the Sovereign LORD says: I am against you, Gog, chief prince of Meshek and Tubal.[4] I will turn you around, put hooks in your jaws and bring you out with your whole army [...].[5] Persia, Cush and Put will be with them [...][6] also Gomer with all its troops, and Beth Togarmah from the far north with all its troops—the many nations with you. [...][14] "Therefore, son of man, prophesy and say to Gog: 'This is what the Sovereign LORD says: In that day, when my people Israel are living in safety, will you not take notice of it?[15] You will come from your place in the far north, you and many nations with you [...] a great horde, a mighty army.[16] You will advance against my people Israel like a cloud that covers the land. In days to come, Gog, I will bring you against my land, so that the nations may know me when I am proved holy through you before their eyes. [...][22] I will execute judgment on him with plague and bloodshed; I will pour down torrents of rain, hailstones and burning sulfur on him and on his troops and on the many nations with him.

Ezekiel 38.2–6.14–16.22

Some dispensationalists take Ezekiel's figure of Gog to be a reference to Russia,[35] as it is stated that Gog's country is in the "far north." It is believed that in the last days Russia will lead a coalition of nations in an attack against the State of Israel. However, according to the biblical account, God will destroy Gog, Magog, and the nations aligned with them, with fire from the heavens before they could even launch their attack against Israel. God would therefore protect the Jewish people against those seeking their destruction. For LaHaye and Jenkins, the war of Gog and Magog against Israel is a significant sign of the end times; it is also a precursor to the rapture of the Church*.

Laurie and Stone believed that Soleimani's assassination was connected to Ezekiel 38, which mentions Persia (now called Iran) as part of the coalition of nations (see Ezekiel 38.5). They interpreted this as having eschatological significance and suggested that the General's assassination could have geo-political consequences for the Middle East, creating the conditions for the Gog and Magog coalition against Israel.

The figure of Gog has been used for various political purposes. During the Cold War in the 1970s and 1980s, the name was mainly associated with Russia. In 2003, President George W. Bush used Gog and Magog to justify the U.S. invasion of Iraq. Today, with Vladimir Putin in Russia and his involvement in Eastern Europe and the Middle East, the idea of an end-time coalition led by the Russians against the Jewish State is re-emerging. Gog and Magog are regaining attention.

Victorious Eschatology: A Different Understanding of the "End Times"

There is another way to interpret the death of Soleimani and the Iranian–American conflict. Some people understand these and other events through the lens of "victorious eschatology."[36] In this paradigm, the expansion of the Kingdom of God will be seen worldwide.[37] The Church* will rise in power, in unity, in maturity, and in glory before Christ's return. Victorious eschatology is compatible with historic premillennialism or postmillennialism—two eschatologies which differ from dispensationalism.

Victorious eschatology perfectly aligns with the New Apostolic Reformation's dominion strategy. It motivates Christians to work at establishing God's Kingdom on earth. In his book titled *Dominion!* C. Peter Wagner explained how he changed his view from premillennial dispensationalism to victorious eschatology. He argued that dispensationalism was too pessimistic and that the "Seven Mountain Mandate" for social transformation required a more positive outlook toward the future:

> If, on the other hand, we now believe that God is mandating our involvement in aggressive social transformation, it is obvious that we will arrive at a different viewpoint. We no longer accept the idea that society will get worse and worse, because we now believe God's mandate is to transform society, so it gets better and better. [...] Victorious eschatology fits dominion theology like a hand in a glove.[38]

In reality, "dominion" can be adapted to different millennial views,[39] either pre-, post-, or even amillennialism.[40] The New Apostolic Reformation welcomes all who wish to participate in their social transformation strategy.

Whether one holds to a historic premillennialist or a postmillennialist eschatological perspective, victorious eschatology helps to better understand the triumphalist attitude of some believers following the attack on Soleimani. For some, the geopolitical upheaval in the Middle East caused by the death of the Iranian general is the consequence of a spiritual war between "territorial spirits" who exert their influence over geographic regions and entire populations.[41] In this view, the American strike on Soleimani would suggest that divine forces have destabilized the "Prince of Persia" (as mentioned in Daniel 10.12–21), which is the "territorial spirit" over Iran. In October 2019, Lance Wallnau had a conversation with Rick Ridings in Jerusalem. Ridings is the founder of Succat Hallel ("house of praise"), a ministry in Jerusalem dedicated to prayer. During their discussion, Ridings shared a vision he had about "lightning hitting a throne of wickedness."[42] Ridings claimed that on September 9, 2019, God gave him a vision regarding the death of Soleimani. In his vision, Ridings heard "the voice of the Lord going out as lightning to strike demonic thrones over Iran, Russia, and Turkey,"[43] three lightning bolts aimed at defeating the evil principalities over the capitals of these three nations.[44] With a view to the book of Daniel, Wallnau even suggested that Soleimani's death could lead to retaliation from the "Principality of Persia," i.e., the "territorial spirit" over the country. He thought this retaliation could potentially impact Trump's personal property. Wallnau urged believers to pray for the protection of the president and his properties.[45]

Christians engaged in spiritual warfare play their role in the Church's* end-times triumph. This is victorious eschatology in action.

Notes

1 See Luca Trenta, « Élimination de Ghassem Soleimani: une dangereuse escalade dans la politique américaine d'assassinats ciblés »: https://theconversation.com/elimination-de-ghassem-soleimani-une-dangereuse-escalade-dans-la-politique-americaine-dassassinats-cibles-129308/ (accessed 29 May 2023).
2 Vahid Yücesoy, « Assassinat de Suleimani: malgré l'apparente unanimité, l'Iran est plus divisé que jamais »: https://theconversation.com/assassinat-de-suleimani-malgre-apparente-unanimite-liran-est-plus-divise-que-jamais-129406/ (accessed 29 May 2023).
3 https://americanevangelicals.com/wp-content/uploads/2018/09/Evangelical-Leaders-Applaud-President-Trump-on-Jerusalem-Jan.-4-2018.pdf (accessed 11 April 2020).
4 See Paul O'Donnell, "For some, the US Embassy's move to Jerusalem fulfills divine prophecy": https://religionnews.com/2018/05/14/some-christians-and-jews-hail-embassy-move-to-jerusalem-as-key-to-a-biblical-plan/ (accessed 29 May 2023).
5 N = 1,997. LifeWay Research is a Baptist research institute serving churches and located in Nashville, Tennessee; see https://lifewayresearch.com/ (accessed 29 May 2023).
6 https://lifewayresearch.com/wp-content/uploads/2017/12/Evangelical-Attitudes-Toward-Israel-Research-Study-Report.pdf (accessed 29 May 2023).
7 Aline Jaccottet, « Un plan de paix marqué par les chrétiens sionistes »: https://www.reformes.ch/politique/2020/01/un-plan-de-paix-marque-par-les-chretiens-sionistes-israel-palestine-politique/ (accessed 29 May 2023).
8 https://templeinstitute.org/statement-of-principles-2/ (accessed 29 May 2023).
9 Note that the institute also works at manufacturing and restoring sacred objects for service in the Temple; see https://www.facebook.com/pg/templeinstitute/about/ (accessed 29 May 2023).
10 See https://templeinstitute.org/about-us/ (accessed 29 May 2023).
11 See Julie Ingersoll, "Why Trump's Evangelical Supporters Welcome His Move on Jerusalem": https://theconversation.com/why-trumps-evangelical-supporters-welcome-his-move-on-jerusalem-88775/ (accessed 29 May 2023).
12 See https://www.youtube.com/watch?v=sO0opXYM52w&feature=youtu.be/ (accessed 09 April 2020).
13 Some people may also combine elements from different paradigms; see Gregg (1997) and Pate, Gentry, Jr., Hamstra, and Thomas (1998).
14 See Nel (2015).
15 For a detailed history of the origins of dispensationalism, see Bass (2005).

16 The Plymouth Brethren are an evangelical movement originating in Dublin at the beginning of the 19th century.

17 Dispensationalism usually divides biblical history into seven "dispensations": (1) innocence, before the sin of Adam; (2) conscience, from the time of Adam to Noah; (3) human government, from Noah to Abraham; (4) the patriarchs, from Abraham to Moses; (5) the mosaic law, from Moses to Christ; (6) grace, the present time, the era of the Church*; and (7) the millennial reign to come.

18 "15[50] I declare to you, brothers and sisters, that flesh and blood cannot inherit the kingdom of God, nor does the perishable inherit the imperishable. [51] Listen, I tell you a mystery: We will not all sleep, but we will all be changed— [52] in a flash, in the twinkling of an eye, at the last trumpet. For the trumpet will sound, the dead will be raised imperishable, and we will be changed. [53] For the perishable must clothe itself with the imperishable, and the mortal with immortality" (1 Cor. 15.50–53). This New Testament text is used in support this view.

19 The precise moment of the rapture of the Church* has some variants. In brief, some claim that the "rapture" will come before the "seven-year tribulation"; known as pretribulationism. Others are of the opinion that the believers will be "raptured" to heaven in the middle of the "seven-year tribulation," i.e., after three and one-half years; referred to as mid-tribulationism. There are also those subscribing to the theory of "prewrath rapture," which takes place near the middle of the second half of the "seven-year tribulation." Finally, there are the post-tribulationists who see the "rapture" taking place at the end of the "seven-year tribulation." For more details, see https://www.pre-trib.org/ (accessed 29 May 2023), as well as Kemp (1991) and Rosenthal (1990).

20 For more details, see McClain (2010).

21 Dispensationalists argue for two possible dates for the decree to rebuild Jerusalem, either 458 BCE, during the seventh year of the reign of King Artaxerxes (see Ezra 7.7–8) or during the twentieth year of his reign in 444 BCE (see Neh. 2.1).

22 Dispensationalists add 483 years—supposing, of course, that one year corresponds to 360 days, which is not necessarily the case—to the decree ordering the reconstruction of Jerusalem. Their calculations bring them approximately to the years 32 or 33 CE, the time they claim when Jesus of Nazareth was crucified in Jerusalem.

23 "The middle of the week" would be 3-1/2 years.

24 According to dispensationalists, the Antichrist will sit in the Temple, desecrate it, and proclaim himself God (see 2 Thess. 2.4). It will be "the abomination that causes desolation" of which is spoken in the Gospels of Mark and Matthew (see Mark 13.14; Matt. 24.15).

25 See Eberle and Trench (2006).

26 Lindsey (1970).

27 Hal Lindsey is an American evangelist, author, and Christian television host. He has dedicated himself to the study of biblical prophecies from a dispensational, pretribulational, and premillennial perspective.

28 See the complete series in the references: LaHaye and Jenkins (1995), (1996), (1997), (1999a), (1999b), (1999c), (2000a), (2000b), (2001), (2002), (2003), (2004), (2005a), (2005b), (2006), (2007).

29 For the following information, see Robert D. McFadden, "Tim LaHaye Dies at 90; Fundamentalist Leader's Grisly Novels Sold Millions": https://www.nytimes.com/2016/07/26/books/tim-lahaye-a-christian-fundamentalist-leader-dies-at-90.html/ (accessed 29 May 2023).

30 LaHaye and Jenkins (2006).

31 See the "author's note" at the end of his prequel: LaHaye and Jenkins (2006, pp. 347–351).

32 LaHaye and Jenkins (2005b).

33 Greg Laurie is the senior pastor of Harvest Christian Fellowship in California.

34 See Laurie's discussions on this subject: https://youtu.be/xbLTvWkxzWg/ (accessed 29 May 2023) and from Stone: https://youtu.be/pX4fSM24mJA/ (accessed 29 May 2023).

35 The identification of Gog and Magog with Russia was popularized in the context of the Cold War by Hal Lindsey, with the publication of his book on eschatology: *The Late Great Planet Earth* in 1970.

36 See Eberle and Trench (2006).

37 Eberle and Trench (2006, p. 1).

38 Wagner (2008, p. 61).

39 For the different eschatological perspectives associated with dominion, see the following infographic: https://adioma.com/@ChristianRightXposed/infographic/what-is-christian-dominionism/ (accessed 29 May 2023).

40 According to amillennialism, there is no "millennium"; everything related to the "millennium" is interpreted symbolically without reference to history. Such a perspective adopts an idealist interpretive paradigm.

41 See the preceding chapter on spiritual warfare.

42 https://lancewallnau.com/spiritual-warfare-alert-how-to-pray/ (accessed 28 May 2023).

43 https://succathallel.com/how-to-pray-after-the-soleimani-assassination/ (accessed 28 May 2023).

44 https://succathallel.com/lightning-confirms-proclamations-over-turkey-russia-and-iran/ (accessed 28 May 2023).

45 https://lancewallnau.com/trump-properties-targeted/ (accessed 28 May 2023).

CONCLUSION

In America today, there are contemporary Charismatic leaders and their followers who seek political power and view former President Trump as "chosen by God," similar to a modern-day Cyrus. Though they may deny it, Trump has given weight to their fantasy of a society based on divine right. The idea echoes the theocratic order from Old Testament stories, where political figures exercised power by divine decree. These Christians firmly believe that Trump had been put in power by divine will, making it difficult for them to criticize the former president's political actions and the record of his administration.

Some evangelical Christians continue to support this former president, who has a reputation for corruption and lies, while others are dismayed by his immoral behavior. The former editor-in-chief of *Christianity Today* had even called for Trump's removal. There is, however, a subset of Charismatic Christians who defend "their" president fervently, extol their political theology of power, and are deeply drawn to *power* itself. Their predictions, visions, decrees, and manifestations of divine authority all embody a fascination with *absolute power*. These preachers tend to focus heavily on Old Testament stories featuring politically powerful figures like Joshua, David, and Cyrus, whose power God had conferred upon them.

The infatuation that Charismatic Trump-supporting leaders have with powerful figures is an essential departure from early Pentecostalism. These Charismatics construct their political theology from the Old Testament, where access to power is often depicted through stories of war and conquest, and where kings and leaders were "chosen by God." Conversely, early 20th-century Pentecostal leaders were focused on restoring the Church as described in the New Testament. While contemporary Trump-supporting Charismatics

DOI: 10.4324/9781003358718-6

also value the idea of restoration, it is secondary to their use of theocratic, prophetic, priestly, and royal imagery from the Old Testament to support their quest for dominion.

The vision that these Charismatic leaders have of a Christian hegemony cannot be achieved without a new idea of how the church operates. The New Apostolic Reformation's church model revolves around the restoration of the five-fold ministry (Eph. 4.11–13) and an apostolic system of governance. This model challenges the democratic structures of churches. The New Order of the Latter Rain, which emerged in the late 1940s, also emphasized the five-fold ministry in reaction to the institutionalization of Pentecostal churches. Similarly, the importance that is placed on the authority of apostles resonates with the accountability model of the Shepherding/Discipleship movement in the early days of the Charismatic renewal, where believers were to submit to the guidance of a "shepherd" responsible for their well-being.

As we have seen, Trump-supporting Charismatics also appeal to the New Testament to validate the authority of their apostles and prophets, as well as the existence of their apostolic centers and networks. The idea of restoration in the book of Acts serves first and foremost to justify their strategy of conquering cultural and territorial spheres. As religious and political entrepreneurs, these apostles view society through a marketing lens. They operate as "trainers" and "marketing" agents with their teams—"apostles in the workplace"—to capture territorial control from their religious competitors. They seek to take hold of the "spheres" of their enemies by referring to Old Testament accounts of war and conquest to justify their actions. Even apostolic prayer networks are mobilized toward political action as a means of achieving their social transformation goals.

The "third wave of the Spirit" has successfully combined elements of the "Pentecostal experience" and the Charismatic renewal. Wagner and Wallnau have expanded this "wave" toward new possibilities. The "Seven Mountain Mandate" has become the sociopolitical transformation project of Wagner's New Apostolic Reformation. These Charismatics leaders have "pentecostalized" Rushdoony's Christian Reconstruction project for dominion by transforming and infusing it with typical Pentecostal dynamism. We are now witnessing the integration of a new theology of power even among Pentecostals. Some predict the emergence of a "fourth wave of the Spirit."[1] It remains to be seen how much of an impact this new "wave" will have.[2]

The growth of Pentecostalism has been remarkable since the beginning of the 20th century, and it continues to expand through the other "waves of the Spirit." The scope of a new "wave" could be unprecedented. Currently, according to the Center for the Study of Global Christianity,[3] there are 680 million Pentecostals/Charismatics worldwide, which is equivalent to one-quarter of the world's 2.6 billion Christians. It is estimated that between 2010 and 2020, an average of 55,000 people joined the ranks of this movement per day, with an annual increase of about 20 million. By 2050, it is estimated that the number of Pentecostals/Charismatics worldwide will reach one billion, making up one-third of the world's Christians. If Charismatic leaders carry their political theology of power into this "fourth wave," its impact could be felt globally.

These Charismatic leaders showed unwavering support for Trump and for his policies and viewed any opposition to the former president as spiritual warfare. They stigmatized and delegitimized their critics, claiming their enemies to be under demonic influence. These enemies include political and religious leaders who do not share the same enthusiasm for Trump and his vision for the United States. Some Charismatics have even prophesized the coming of a second American civil war—encouraging Christians to defend themselves against all opposition to Trump and their plan for a Christian hegemony. Many of these Trump-supporting Charismatics view democratic pluralism with suspicion and often try to silence church leaders who disagree with them. Pluralism is simply—and literally—demonized. This is still clearly seen in their rejection of mainstream media coverage of scientific news related to global climate change, or to COVID-19,[4] for example. These apostles and prophets immediately denounce such media reports as conspiracies and refuse to engage in any discussion. Those who adopt a different perspective are utterly demonized.

Charismatic supporters of Trump are also deeply concerned about the end of the world. We have seen how biblical prophecies are read through the prism of political events. Whether it be Russia represented by Gog and Magog, the Iranian-American conflict understood as the stirring of a "territorial spirit," or the role of Jerusalem and the fantasy of its Temple's reconstruction, these and other events are seen as signs of the end times. This futuristic interpretation of biblical texts seeks to connect Bible prophecies to contemporary geopolitics. Currently, this eschatological outlook weighs heavily on the U.S. relationship with the modern State of Israel. By strictly favoring Israeli policies, the American stance proves to be harmful to the Palestinian community and undermines the peace process. The Christian right's influence on political power constitutes a menace not only for the United States, but also for world stability.

How can we address this situation? While taking action is important, it is crucial to conduct a proper analysis beforehand. Rushing into action without prior analysis is doomed to fail. To make progress, decision-makers, political leaders, and the general public should strive to reach a deeper understanding of these religious groups. Scholarly research on these questions must be precise—painting too broad a picture of these groups is likely to be counterproductive, failing to provide a precise critique and running the risk of exacerbating tensions. The work of collecting information relative to the origins, beliefs, practices, and political inclinations of Charismatics, Pentecostals, and evangelicals in general is necessary.

All too often, due to a lack of information, the mainstream media furthers the impression that *all* evangelicals supported Trump. It's not just journalists who are involved in this issue. Evangelical leaders, regardless of their specific faith tradition (Baptist, Reformed, Holiness, Pentecostal, Charismatic, etc.), must have the courage to speak out against the political views of Christians who endorsed the former president, just as Mark Galli did.[5] These leaders need to reject the idea of a Christian-dominated society that demonizes political, social, and religious opponents and uses eschatology to influence U.S. geopolitical positions. Encouraging them to take such a stand does not mean they have to deny their convictions or adopt a more liberal theology. Instead, it means urging them to promote democratic pluralism within the evangelical community and to help create a society respectful of pluralism, capable of critical debate, and tolerant of the diversity of morals and values.

Labeling the beliefs of these ultra-conservative religious leaders and their followers as "irrational" or "crazy" poses a risk to the general public. And what does one gain by doing so? This type of language can lead to infantilization and push them to adopt even more radical positions. It's important to try to understand the fundamental roots of actions which have religious motives, even if we remain agnostic about what is beyond. Instead of exacerbating a binary worldview, we should seek to bring about change through understanding and avoid the delusion of an "us" versus "them" mentality which just confirms and feeds into a mutual sense of persecution.

The mainstream media has the responsibility to expose the negative impact of erroneous theological ideas on democracy, diversity, and religious freedom. To achieve this, journalists and major news outlets need to accurately portray the social and ideological complexities of these religious groups by relying on scholarly expertise. It is important to avoid misrepresenting their views or assuming negative intentions without evidence.

The polarization of American society is a concerning issue. It is up to us to decide whether we want to add to this divide or to strive to communicate and engage in dialog whenever possible—with the hope that it can still be achieved.

Notes

1 See J. W. Goll, "The Fourth Great Wave of the Holy Spirit Has Begun": https://charismamag.com/blogs/a-voice-calling-out/the-fourth-great-wave-of-the-holy-spirit-has-begun/ (accessed 29 May 2023).
2 Surprisingly, some non-charismatic evangelical factions now also reference the "Seven Mountains" of culture; see P. Montgomery, "Southern Baptist Convention's National Day of Prayer Guide Uses Seven Mountains Framework": https://www.rightwingwatch.org/post/southern-baptist-conventions-national-day-of-prayer-guide-uses-seven-mountains-framework/ (accessed 29 May 2023).

3 "Status of Global Christianity, 2023, in the Context of 1900-2050": https://www.gordonconwell.edu/wp-content/uploads/sites/13/2023/01/Status-of-Global-Christianity-2023.pdf (accessed 29 May 2023).
4 On the reactions of some Charismatics leaders to the pandemic, see Gagné (2022).
5 For example, this has been the initiative of groups like "Christians Against Christian Nationalism"; see https://www.christiansagainstchristiannationalism.org/ (accessed 29 May 2023).

EPILOGUE

On November 3, 2020, Donald Trump lost his bid for re-election. This loss went against everything most pro-Trump prophets had predicted.[1] The Neocharismatic-Pentecostal world was in turmoil.[2] How could so many people get it wrong?[3] How could they have misinterpreted what they "heard from God"? Several rationalizations were given, either to salvage the prophets or to salvage Trump himself.

Stolen Election and Failed Prophecies

Perhaps the most common justification was that the election had been stolen by the Democrats. Trump had already invoked the possibility during the campaign that the election would be rigged, and his supporters bought into the "Big Lie."[4] Mike Lindell, the *My Pillow* CEO, claimed to have proof that the election was stolen. In a series of documentaries, Lindell argued that "foreign hackers broke into the computer systems of election offices like Clark County to switch votes – in what he has described as the 'biggest cyber-crime in world history.'"[5] Despite the fact that Lindell's claims have consistently been disproved, many Republicans[6] and evangelical Trump-supporting leaders[7] continued to believe in the "Big Lie."

Another reason given to explain the failure of prophecy and Trump's election loss was that prophets are not infallible; they can sometimes get it wrong. In response to people who labeled failed prophecies as being the mark of false prophets (see Deuteronomy 13.1–5), Craig Keener, a professor of Biblical Studies at Asbury Seminary, wrote that "mistakes in prophecy do not make everyone who's mistaken a false prophet."[8] Keener apologetically explained that prophecies need to be evaluated, and Christians are to retain

DOI: 10.4324/9781003358718-7

what is good and reject what is evil (see 1 Corinthians 14.29 and 1 Thessalonians 5.19–22). Accordingly, Keener believes that prophets and their prophecies, at least in the context of the New Testament, could err. He notes, however, that mistaken predictions are harmful for the Church.

Some prophets claimed that Trump was not re-elected because he needed to go through what they called his "Nebuchadnezzar moment." Prophets Jennifer LeClaire[9] and Jeremiah Johnson[10] both believed that God was calling Trump to repent of his pride, just as had King Nebuchadnezzar of old (see Daniel 4). Even Trump's spiritual advisor, Paula White-Cain, after having engaged in active prayer meetings at her church to ask God to expose the corruption behind the election results and to overturn the election if necessary,[11] complained to her own spiritual father, Archbishop Nicholas Duncan-Williams, about Trump's sinful actions and stubbornness.[12]

It is clear that the failed Trump prophecies have caused a rift among NCPs.[13] "The Prophetic Standards,"[14] a statement signed by 92 Charismatic leaders in April 2021, addressed the issue of prophets who engage in political predictions. This effort by certain Charismatic leaders to clarify their stance on political prophecies has had some, albeit limited, success. Out of some 40 prophets who predicted a second term for Trump, a few admitted that they were wrong, among them Jeremiah Johnson, R. Loren Sandford, Kris Valloton, and Shawn Bolz.[15] Others continue to claim that God revealed to them that Trump is the true elected president.[16]

The Damage Was Done

Rationalizations aside, Trump's "Big Lie" had its desired effect in the minds of most Republicans and many evangelical Trump supporters. The damage was done. Many believed that Biden was an illegitimately elected president, and they would do whatever was necessary to prevent the congressional certification of the Electoral College votes on January 6, 2021. The build-up to a January 6, 2021, insurrection had been growing since the election. A series of protests began the day following the election, on November 4, in various cities across the United States. On November 12, 2020, thousands of protesters, including far-right leader Alex Jones and militia groups, such as the Proud Boys and the Oath Keepers, attended the "March for Trump" event in Washington, D.C.[17]

One month later, on December 12, 2020, a "Stop the Steal" rally and a "Jericho March" were held in the nation's capital.[18] "Jericho Marches" are inspired by the biblical story one reads in Chapter 6 of the book of Joshua, where the ancient Israelites are ordered by God to march around the evil city of Jericho for seven days, all the while praying, worshiping, and blowing Shofars,[19] believing that the city walls would crumble and they would capture and kill their enemies. The December 12, 2020, "Jericho March" rally was emceed by evangelical Trump ally Eric Metaxas. A mix of Trump-supporting Christian leaders and far-right groups were at the event. Speakers included as follows: Jonathan Cahn, Leon Benjamin, Lance Wallnau, Michele Bachmann, Mike Lindell, General Michael Flynn, Archbishop Carlo Maria Viganò, Ali Alexander, and Alex Jones, to name a few.[20] Other "Jericho Marches" were also held that same day in Georgia, Pennsylvania, Michigan, Wisconsin, Nevada, and Arizona—all "battleground" states, most of which had flipped from Republican to Democrat in the election.[21]

The "Stop the Steal" crowd and the "Jericho Marchers" were back in Washington, D.C., on January 5, 2021. This time actions would speak louder than words[22]: the following day, the world would witness the insurrection at the very seat of American government, the United States Capitol complex.[23] From Saturday, January 2, to Monday, January 4, self-guided "Jericho Marches" were scheduled around the U.S. Capitol or the Supreme Court. On Tuesday, January 5, a Shofar blown and guided "Jericho March" around the Supreme Court began at noon. On the same day, a "One Nation Under God" prayer rally[24] was organized near the Supreme Court. At noon on the day of the insurrection, another Jericho March was called around the U.S. Capitol with the blowing of Shofars. A "Stop the Steal" rally was organized from 10 a.m. to 5 p.m. on Capitol Hill, and more importantly, Trump gave a speech at a "Save America Rally" at The Ellipse from 11:58 a.m. to 1:12 p.m. The attack began at 1:03 p.m., and by 1:12 p.m., an estimated 8,000 people were moving up the Mall even before Trump finished his speech.[25] During the insurrection, banners marked with "Jesus Saves" and "Jesus 2020" flew alongside QAnon flags bearing the slogan WWG1WGA (Where We Go One, We Go All).

Scholars on Twitter using the hashtag #CapitolSiegeReligion[26] and on various websites cataloged online images, references, and gestures.[27] Clearly, some Christians were involved in the insurrection, as they believed both Trump's "Big Lie" and that the Democrats were the sworn enemies of their faith. Not only had Trump conditioned his supporters prior to the election to believe he could lose due to a corrupt electoral process, but also the immediate organization of rallies such as "Stop the Steal" and the various "Jericho" marches were the radicalizing ingredients that pushed some of the former president's Christian supporters to be involved in an event that nearly overturned the democratic order in the United States.

As discussed throughout this book, in the months leading to the election, some of Trump's loyal evangelical leaders, such as Franklin Graham, Paula White-Cain, and Lance Wallnau, had expressed hostile views through their contentious religious rhetoric. What was believed about Trump being God's "Chosen One" could have led some Christians to embrace the "Big Lie" and engage in the insurrection. As we saw, many conservative Christians were warning of an impending second American civil war. At the December 12, 2020, rally, Lance Wallnau spoke of the rise of a Christian populist movement whose presence would be felt in the coming years. It would seem that the insurrection could not have happened without this Christian populist movement, joining efforts with far-right leaders and groups.

Trump's Other Sociopolitical Legacies

The consequences of Trump's Presidency and "Big Lie" run deep. Admittedly, Trump did accomplish several things which pleased his evangelical voters.[28] For evangelicals, one of his most important accomplishments was the appointment of three conservative judges to the Supreme Court during his term: Neil Gorsuch in 2017, Brett Cavanaugh in 2018, and Amy Coney Barrett in 2020.[29] These appointments changed the balance of the Court and greatly facilitated the reversal of *Roe v. Wade*, for which Trump took credit.[30] There has been, however, a reported drop in evangelical support for Trump's presidential bid in 2024. The former president has qualified the evangelical's lack of support as a mark of disloyalty, saying

> nobody has ever done more for Right to Life than Donald Trump. I put three Supreme Court justices, who all voted, and they got something that they've been fighting for 64 years, for many, many years ... There's great disloyalty in the world of politics and that's a sign of disloyalty.[31]

The impact of the "Big Lie" not only resulted in the January 6, 2021, insurrection but also in a continuing effort among evangelicals, conservative Catholics, far-right factions, and conspiracy groups to pursue their fight for America. Clay Clark, for example, organized the popular ReAwaken America Tour, a series of country-wide political protests sponsored by *Charisma News*.[32] Initially established in reaction to the COVID-19 government policies, the Tour has also been promoting spiritual warfare, QAnon conspiracies, America as a Christian nation, the Great Reset conspiracy, etc. It has garnered the participation of former General Michael Flynn, Roger Stone, Mark Burns, and Greg Locke, to name a few.

The 2022 mid-term elections also saw the advent of numerous candidates supporting the former president and seeking his endorsement. Among the key electoral races was the Pennsylvania gubernatorial race, pitting Republican candidate Doug Mastriano against Democrat Josh Shapiro. There were a plethora of stories about Mastriano on topics ranging from his presence at the Capitol on January 6[33] to his close ties with some political prophets such as Julie Green and key New Apostolic Reformation leader in Pennsylvania, Abby Abildness.[34] After his loss to Shapiro, Mastriano continued to fuel his supporters and is prayerfully contemplating a run for Republican senator in Pennsylvania in 2024.[35] During the 2022 mid-terms, Trump "endorsed over

330 candidates, held 30 rallies, and raised millions of dollars," but many of his major picks did not win.[36] Adding to Trump's legal problems[37] are his political troubles. In 2022, Ron DeSantis, the successful Florida governor, was seen by some conservatives as a better Republican candidate for the 2024 presidential elections.[38]

At the time of this writing, Trump is still leading as the Republican 2024 preferred candidate,[39] despite having been found liable for sexually abusing and defaming writer E. Jean Carroll in a civil trial.[40] Trump has also been indicted in June 2023 for taking classified documents from the White House after he left office,[41] and most recently, on 1 August 2023, he was indicted for his efforts to overturn the 2020 election.[42] Regardless of these serious multiple charges, the former president has the continued support of the most extreme remnant of Christian voters inspired by Charismatic dominionism, modern-day prophecy, and conspiratorial thinking—more specifically those involved in the ReAwaken America Tour.[43] Will the leaders pushing the political theology of power I describe in this book manage to mobilize Trump-supporting evangelicals once more, resulting in his victory in the 2024 elections? In light of the political damage following Trump's election in 2016, his debacle for re-election in 2020, his persistence in lying about the election results, his tenacity in wanting to recapture the White House, and his willingness to pardon most of the January 6 insurrectionists,[44] one may ask if the democratic institutions in the United States are in jeopardy. Are American voters at an impasse? Is this a point of no return? Only time will tell whether the foundations of American democracy will withstand the assault and undermining by one man and those who support him, or if these pillars will crumble under the weight of their constant aggression.

Notes

1 See https://www.politico.com/news/magazine/2021/02/18/how-christian-prophets-give-credence-to-trumps-election-fantasies-469598 (accessed 29 May 2023).
2 See Paul Djupe's data on the number of Americans who believe in modern-day prophets and prophecy: https://religioninpublic.blog/2023/04/10/how-many-americans-believe-in-modern-day-prophets-what-does-that-entail/ (accessed 29 May 2023).
3 See https://pcpj.org/2020/12/15/these-12-church-leaders-prophesied-that-trump-would-win-the-2020-election/ (accessed 29 May 2023).
4 On what gave rise to the "Big Lie," see https://www.cnn.com/2021/05/19/politics/donald-trump-big-lie-explainer/index.html (accessed 29 May 2023).
5 See CNN's report on Lindell's claims: https://www.cnn.com/2021/08/05/politics/mike-lindell-mypillow-ceo-election-claims-invs/index.html (accessed 29 May 2023).
6 Many Republicans still believe in the "Big Lie," see https://www.washingtonpost.com/politics/2022/09/28/nearly-700-days-later-most-republicans-still-believe-trumps-big-lie/ (accessed 29 May 2023).
7 See https://www.nytimes.com/2022/04/25/us/politics/evangelical-churches-trump-election.html (accessed 29 May 2023).

8 See Keener's apologetic article in *Christianity Today*: https://www.christianitytoday.com/ct/2020/november-web-only/political-prophecy-false-bible-scholar-trump-election.html (accessed 29 May 2023).

9 See LeClaire's view on Trump's missed re-election: https://365prophetic.com/2020/11/05/trump-prophecy-president-faces-a-nebuchadnezzar-moment/ (accessed 29 May 2023).

10 Johnson on the danger of Trump becoming a "Nebuchadnezzar" because of his pride: https://christiannews.net/2021/01/11/idolatry-jeremiah-johnson-receives-death-threats-from-trump-supporters-for-apologizing-over-election-prophecy/ (accessed 29 May 2023).

11 See https://religiondispatches.org/beneath-the-wacky-paula-white-video-is-a-dark-and-deeply-undemocratic-world-propping-up-the-president/ (accessed 29 May 2023).

12 Report on White-Cain's comments: https://www.ghanaweb.com/GhanaHomePage/NewsArchive/Duncan-Williams-no-longer-friends-with-stubborn-Trump-Owusu-Bempah-1101208 (accessed 29 May 2023).

13 See my co-written piece with Clarkson on the rift caused by the mistaken Trump prophecies: https://religiondispatches.org/new-apostolic-reformation-faces-profound-rift-due-to-trump-prophecies-and-spiritual-manipulation-of-the-prophetic-gift/ (accessed 29 May 2023).

14 For the full statement, see https://propheticstandards.com (accessed 29 May 2023).

15 For more on those who recognized their error and those who did not, see https://baysidechurch.com.au/blog/and-the-prophets-apologise-a-little/ (accessed 29 May 2023).

16 Among those who claimed such things are Prophets Kat Kerr and Hank Kunneman: https://religionunplugged.com/news/2021/1/12/charismatics-are-at-war-with-each-other-over-failed-prophecies-of-trump-victory (accessed 29 May 2023).

17 See https://www.bbc.com/news/world-us-canada-54945154 (accessed 29 May 2023).

18 See https://www1.cbn.com/cbnnews/us/2020/december/we-come-in-faith-to-our-god-millions-watch-as-jericho-marchers-march-on-nations-capital (accessed 29 May 2023).

19 On the significance of Shofar blowing, see Leah Payne's insightful article: https://politicaltheology.com/the-trump-shall-sound-politics-pentecostals-and-the-shofar-at-the-capitol-riots/ (accessed 29 May 2023).

20 For more on the 12 December 2020 "Jericho March," see https://religionunplugged.com/news/2020/12/13/trump-supporting-jericho-march-ends-in-protest (accessed 29 May 2023).

21 See https://www.dw.com/en/pro-trump-election-protests-descend-into-violent-clashes/a-55920453 (accessed 29 May 2023).

22 Read Jordan Green's piece on how "Jericho March" extremists point to the threat of MAGA violence: https://www.rawstory.com/raw-investigates/trump-extremists-2660264511/ (accessed 29 May 2023).

23 For the schedule of events preceding the January 6, 2021, Capitol insurrection, see https://uncivilreligion.org/home/media/320.jpg (accessed 29 May 2023).

24 This prayer rally was hosted by Virginia Women for Trump and in collaboration with Stop the Steal, AmericanPhoenix.org, and Jericho March; see https://www.hillrag.com/2021/01/06/where-are-wednesdays-pro-trump-protests/ (accessed 29 May 2023).

25 See https://web.archive.org/web/20210118180312/https://www.newyorker.com/magazine/2021/01/25/among-the-insurrectionists (accessed 29 May 2023).

26 For example, see Peter Manseau's Twitter handle (@plmanseau) and threads on #CapitolSiegeReligion.

27 See the website Uncivil Religion (https://uncivilreligion.org/home/index) with its important repertoire of images, sounds, documents, and videos of crowds, people, rituals, signs, and symbols during the Capitol attack (accessed 29 May 2023).

28 Here are few examples according to the Christian Post: https://www.christianpost.com/news/7-trump-accomplishments-evangelicals-like.html?page=1 (accessed 29 May 2023).

29 See https://www.senate.gov/legislative/nominations/SupremeCourtNominations 1789present.htm (accessed 29 May 2023).

30 Trump was quick to take credit for the reversal of *Roe v. Wade*, saying this would not have been possible before and was "only made possible because I delivered everything as promised, including nominating and getting three highly respected and strong Constitutionalists confirmed to the United States Supreme Court"; see https://www.cnbc.com/2022/06/24/roe-v-wade-decision-trump-takes-credit-for-supreme-court-abortion-ruling.html (accessed 29 May 2023).

31 See https://www.cnn.com/2023/01/18/politics/donald-trump-evangelicals-2024/index.html (accessed 29 May 2023).

32 For details, dates, and sponsors, see https://www.thrivetimeshow.com/reawaken-america-tour/ (accessed 29 May 2023).

33 See https://www.nbcnews.com/politics/2022-election/trumps-pick-pennsylvania-governor-says-sees-parallels-hitlers-power-gr-rcna33167 (accessed 29 May 2023).

34 Fred Clarkson wrote an important piece on the ties between Abildness and Mastriano: https://www.salon.com/2022/07/04/hes-on-a-mission-from-god-pennsylvania-candidate-doug-mastrianos-with-the-world/ (accessed 29 May 2023).

35 In a rare interview with mainstream media, Mastriano said "What do you do with a movement of 2.2 million? We're keeping it alive"; see https://www.politico.com/news/2023/03/07/mastriano-weighing-senate-run-2024-00085747 (accessed 29 May 2023).

36 See https://www.politico.com/news/2022/11/09/trump-endorsed-candidates-2022-election-results (accessed 29 May 2023).

37 For the long list of Trump legal troubles, see https://www.businessinsider.com/donald-trump-key-cases-civil-criminal-investigations-lawsuits-updates-2022-7 (accessed 29 May 2023).

38 See https://www.bbc.com/news/world-us-canada-63967234 (accessed 29 May 2023).

39 Trumps leads DeSantis in an April 2023 poll: https://www.nbcnews.com/meet-the-press/meetthepressblog/trump-leads-desantis-gop-primary-field-new-nbc-poll-rcna81141 (accessed 29 May 2023).

40 See https://www.nbcnews.com/politics/donald-trump/jury-reaches-verdict-e-jean-carroll-rape-defamation-case-trump-rcna82778 (accessed 29 May 2023).

41 See https://edition.cnn.com/interactive/2023/07/politics/trump-indictments-criminal-cases/index.html (accessed 1 August 2023).

42 See https://www.nytimes.com/live/2023/08/01/us/trump-indictment-jan-6 (accessed 1 August, 2023).

43 At the time of this writing, the most recent ReAwaken America Tour event was at Trump's Doral Resort in Miami, Florida, on May 12, 2023; for more, see https://momentmag.com/deep-dive-clay-clark-reawaken-america/ (accessed 29 May 2023).

44 If elected, Trump promised to pardon Capitol rioters: https://www.washingtonpost.com/national-security/2022/09/01/trump-jan-6-rioters-pardon/ (accessed 29 May 2023).

BIBLIOGRAPHY

Adelakun, Abimbola A. *Powerful Devices. Prayer and the Political Praxis of Spiritual Warfare*. New Brunswick: Rutgers University Press, 2023.

Ahn, Ché. *Modern-Day Apostles: Operating in Your Apostolic Office and Anointing*. Shippensburg, Pennsylvania: Destiny Image Publishers, 2019.

Anderson, Allen H. *Spreading Fires. The Missionary Nature of Early Pentecostalism*. Maryknoll, New York: Orbis Books, 2007.

Anderson, Allen H. *To the Ends of the Earth. Pentecostalism and the Transformation of World Christianity*. Oxford: Oxford University Press, 2013.

Anderson, Neil T. *Victory over the Darkness: Realize the Power of Your Identity in Christ*. Bloomington, Minnesota: Bethany House, 2000.

Asamoah-Gyadu, J. Kwabena. *African Charismatics. Current Developments within Independent Indigenous Pentecostalism in Ghana* (Studies of Religion in Africa: Supplements to the Journal of Religion in Africa, vol. 27). Boston: Brill, 2005.

Balmer, Randall H. *The Making of Evangelicalism: From Revivalism to Politics and Beyond*. Waco, Texas: Baylor University Press, 2010.

Barr, Beth Allison. *The Making of Biblical Womanhood: How the Subjugation of Woman Became Gospel Truth*. Ada, Michigan: Brazos Press, 2021.

Bartoş, Emil. "The Three Waves of Spiritual Renewal of the Pentecostal-Charismatic Movement." *Review of Ecumenical Studies Sibiu*, 7.1, 2015, pp. 20–42.

Bass, Clarence B. *Backgrounds to Dispensationalism: Its Historical Genesis and Ecclesiastical Implications*. Eugene, Oregon: Wipf & Stock, 2005.

Bassett, Paul Merritt. "The Theological Identity of the North American Holiness Movement: Its Understanding of the Nature and Role of the Bible." *The Variety of American Evangelicalism*. Edited by Donald W. Dayton and Robert K. Johnston. Eugene, Oregon: Wipf & Stock, 1997, pp. 72–108.

Bebbington, David W. *Evangelicalism in Modern Britain: A History from the 1730s to the 1980s*. New York: Routledge, 1989.

Berry, Damon T. *The New Apostolic Reformation, Trump, and Evangelical Politics: The Prophecy Voter*. London: Bloomsbury, 2023.

Bowler, Kate. *Blessed: A History of the American Prosperity Gospel.* Oxford: Oxford University Press, 2013.

Brockschmidt, Annika. *Amerikas Gotteskrieger. Wie die Religiöse Rechte die Demokratie gefährdet.* Hamburg: Rowohlt Verlag GmbH, 2021.

Bruce, Steve. *The Rise and Fall of the New Christian Right: Conservative Protestant Politics in America, 1978–1988.* New York: Clarendon, 1988.

Butler, Anthea. *White Evangelical Racism: The Politics of Morality in America.* Chapel Hill, North Carolina: The University of North Carolina Press, 2021.

Cannistraci, David. *The Gift of Apostle.* Ventura, California: Regal Books, 1996.

Caron, Alain. *Apostolic Centers: Shifting the Church, Transforming the World.* Colorado Springs: Arsenal Press, 2013.

Christerson, Brad and Richard Flory. *The Rise of Network Christianity: How Independent Leaders Are Changing the Religious Landscape.* New York: Oxford University Press, 2017.

Clarkson, Frederick. "Dominionism Rising: A Theocratic Movement Hiding in Plain Sight." *The Public Eye,* Summer, 2016, pp. 12–20.

Compton, John W. *The End of Empathy. Why White Protestants Stopped Loving Their Neighbors.* Oxford: Oxford University Press, 2020.

Cook, Bruce (ed). *Aligning with the Apostolic. Vol. 1-5.* Houston, Texas: Kingdom House Publishing, 2013.

Critchlow, Donald T. *Phyllis Schlafly and Grassroots Conservatism: A Woman's Crusade.* Princeton: Princeton University Press, 2005.

Dayton, Donald W. "Some Doubts about the Usefulness of the Category 'Evangelical.'" *The Variety of American Evangelicalism.* Edited by Donald W. Dayton and Robert K. Johnston. Eugene, Oregon: Wipf & Stock, 1997, pp. 245–251.

Dayton, Donald W. and Douglas M. Strong. *Rediscovering an Evangelical Heritage: A Tradition and Trajectory of Integrating Piety and Justice.* 2nd ed., Grand Rapids, Michigan: Baker Academic, 2014.

Diamond, Sara. *Spiritual Warfare: The Politics of the Christian Right.* Montreal: Black Rose Books, 1990.

Diamond, Sara. *Roads to Dominion: Right-Wing Movements and Political Power in the United States.* New York: Guilford, 1995.

Diamond, Sara. *Not by Politics Alone: The Enduring Influence of the Christian Right.* New York: Guilford, 1998.

Du Mez, Kristin Kobes. *Jesus and John Wayne: How White Evangelicals Corrupted a Faith and Fractured a Nation.* New York: Liveright, 2020.

Eberle, Harold R. and Martin Trench. *Victorious Eschatology: A Partial-Preterist View.* Yakima, Washington: Worldcast Publishing, 2006.

Eckhardt, John. *Deliverance and Spiritual Warfare Manual: A Comprehensive Guide to Living Free.* Lake Mary, Florida: Charisma House, 2014.

Enlow, Johnny. *The Seven Mountain Prophecy: Unveiling the Coming Elijah Revolution.* Lake Mary, Florida: Creation House, 2008.

Enlow, Johnny. *The Seven Mountain Mantle: Receiving the Joseph Anointing to Reform Nations.* Lake Mary, Florida: Creation House, 2009.

Enlow, Johnny. *Seven Mountain Renaissance: Vision and Strategy through 2050.* New Kensington, Pennsylvania: Whitaker House, 2015.

Fairclough, Norman. *Critical Discourse Analysis.* London: Longman, 1995.

Faupel, D. William. *The Everlasting Gospel: The Significance of Eschatology in the Development of Pentecostal Thought*. Sheffield: Sheffield Academic Press, 1996.

Faupel, D. William. "The New Order of the Latter Rain: Restoration or Renewal?" *Winds from the North: Canadian Contributions to the Pentecostal Movement*. Edited by Michael Wilkinson and Peter Althouse. Leiden: Brill, 2010, pp. 239–263.

Fer, Yannick. "Pentecôtisme et modernité urbaine: Entre Déterritorialisation des identités et réinvestissement symbolique de l'espace urbain." *Social Compass*, 54.2, 2007, pp. 201–210.

Fer, Yannick. *L'offensive évangélique. Voyage au cœur des réseaux militants de Jeunesse en Mission*. Geneva: Labor et Fides, 2010.

Fer, Yannick and Philippe Gonzalez. "De Paris à Genève: les lieux communs d'une mobilisation charismatique." *Le protestantisme à Paris*. Edited by Yannick Fer and Gwendoline Malogne-Fer. Geneva: Labor et Fides, 2017, pp. 389–410.

FitzGerald, Frances. *The Evangelicals: The Struggle to Shape America*. New York: Simon and Schuster, 2017.

Gagné, André. "Battling the Plague: Spiritual Warfare, COVID-19, and the Demonization of Political Adversaries." *Religion and Violence in Western Traditions. Selected Studies* (Routledge Studies in Religion). Edited by André Gagné, Jennifer Guyver, and Gerbern S. Oegema. New York: Routledge, 2022, pp. 157–170.

Gagné, André. "The Storming of the Capitol: The Outcome of a Theology of Political Power." *Uncivil Disobedience. Theological Perspectives*. Edited by David M. Gides. Washington, DC: Rowman & Littlefield, 2013, pp. 203–216.

Gonzalez, Philippe. "Lutter contre l'emprise démoniaque: Les politiques du combat spirituel évangélique." *Terrain. Revue d'ethnologie de l'Europe*, 50, 2008, pp. 44–61.

Gonzalez, Philippe. "Défaire le démon, refaire la nation: Le combat spirituel évangélique entre science, religion et politique." *Anges et démon: Actes du colloque de Bastogne*. Edited by Renaud Zeebroek. Bruxelles: Fédération Wallonie-Bruxelles, 2013, pp. 70–100.

Gonzalez, Philippe. *Que ton règne vienne. Des évangéliques tentés par le pouvoir absolu*. Geneva: Labor et Fides, 2014.

Gonzalez, Philippe. "Dieu parle en public. La prophétie charismatique, de l'intimité à la politique." *Pragmata*, 2, 2019, pp. 112–175.

Gorski, Philip and Samuel Perry. *The Flag and the Cross: White Christian Nationalism and the Threat to American Democracy*. Oxford: Oxford University Press, 2022.

Gregg, Steve. *Revelation: Four Views. A Parallel Commentary*. Nashville: Thomas Nelson, 1997.

Hamon Bill. *The Final Reformation and Great Awakening*. Shippensburg, Pennsylvania: Destiny Image Publishers, 2021.

Hardy, Elle. *Beyond Belief: How Pentecostal Christianity Is Taking over the World*. London: Hurst & Co., 2022.

Hart, Darryl G. *Deconstructing Evangelicalism. Conservative Protestantism in the Age of Billy Graham*. Grand Rapids, Michigan: Baker Academic, 2004.

Heale, Michael J. *American Anticommunism: Combating the Enemy Within, 1830-1970*. Baltimore: The John Hopkins University Press, 1990.

Heffer, Jean. *Pourquoi n'y a-t-il pas de socialisme aux États-Unis?* Edited by Jeannine Rovet. Paris: Éditions de l'EHESS, 1988.

Hinn, Costi W. *God, Greed, and the (Prosperity) Gospel: How Truth Overwhelms a Life Built on Lies*. Grand Rapids, Michigan: Zondervan, 2019.

Hofstadter, Richard. *The Paranoid Style in American Politics*. New York: Alfred A. Knopf, 1964.

Holdcroft, L. Thomas. "The New Order of the Latter Rain." *Pneuma*, 2.1, 1980, pp. 46–60.

Holliday, Pat. *Marine Spirits and Mystifying Sea Beings: Marine Demons*. Jacksonville, Florida: Agape Publishers (Deliverance Book 1), 2013a.

Holliday, Pat. *Ruling World Water Spirits: Marine Demons*. Jacksonville, Florida: Agapepublishers (Deliverance Book 2), 2013b.

Holvast, René. *Spiritual Mapping in the United States and Argentina 1989–2005*. Leiden: Brill, 2009.

Hutchinson, Mark. "The Latter Rain Movement and the Phenomenon of Global Return." *Winds from the North: Canadian Contributions to the Pentecostal Movement*. Edited by Michael Wilkinson and Peter Althouse. Leiden: Brill, 2010, pp. 265–283.

Ingersoll, Julie J. *Building God's Kingdom: Inside the World of Christian Reconstruction*. Oxford: Oxford University Press, 2015.

Jackson, Bill. *The Quest for the Radical Middle. A History of the Vineyard*. Cape Town: South Africa: Vineyard International Publishing, 1999.

Jones, Robert P. *White Too Long: The Legacy of White Supremacy in American Christianity*. New York: Simon & Schuster, 2020.

Juergensmeyer, Mark and Mona Kanwal Sheikh. 2013. "A Sociotheological Approach to Understanding Religious Violence." *The Oxford Handbook on Religious Violence*. Edited by Michael Jerryson, Mark Juergensmeyer, and Margo Kitts. Oxford: Oxford University Press, pp. 620–644.

Kemp, Karl. *The Mid-Week Rapture: A Verse-by-Verse Study of Key Prophetic Passages*. Shippensburg, Pennsylvania: Companion Press, 1991.

Kiddie, Tony. *Republican Jesus: How the Right Has Rewritten the Gospels*. Oakland: University of California Press, 2020.

LaHaye, Tim and Jerry B. Jenkins. *Left Behind: A Novel of the Earth's Last Days*. Carol Stream, Illinois: Tyndale House Publishers, 1995.

LaHaye, Tim and Jerry B. Jenkins. *Tribulation Force: The Continuing Drama of Those Left Behind*. Carol Stream, Illinois: Tyndale House Publishers, 1996.

LaHaye, Tim and Jerry B. Jenkins. *Nicolae: The Rise of Antichrist*. Carol Stream, Illinois: Tyndale House Publishers, 1997.

LaHaye, Tim and Jerry B. Jenkins. *Soul Harvest: The World Takes Sides*. Carol Stream, Illinois: Tyndale House Publishers, 1999a.

LaHaye, Tim and Jerry B. Jenkins. *Apollyon: The Destroyer Is Unleashed*. Carol Stream, Illinois: Tyndale House Publishers, 1999b.

LaHaye, Tim and Jerry B. Jenkins. *Assassins: Assignment: Jerusalem, Target: Antichrist*. Carol Stream, Illinois: Tyndale House Publishers, 1999c.

LaHaye, Tim and Jerry B. Jenkins. *The Indwelling: The Beast Takes Possession*. Carol Stream, Illinois: Tyndale House Publishers, 2000a.

LaHaye, Tim and Jerry B. Jenkins. *The Mark: The Beast Rules the World*. Carol Stream, Illinois: Tyndale House Publishers, 2000b.

LaHaye, Tim and Jerry B. Jenkins. *Desecration: Antichrist Takes the Throne*. Carol Stream, Illinois: Tyndale House Publishers, 2001.

LaHaye, Tim and Jerry B. Jenkins. *The Remnant: On the Brink of Armageddon*. Carol Stream, Illinois: Tyndale House Publishers, 2002.

LaHaye, Tim and Jerry B. Jenkins. *Armageddon: The Cosmic Battle of the Ages.* Carol Stream, Illinois: Tyndale House Publishers, 2003.

LaHaye, Tim and Jerry B. Jenkins. *Glorious Appearing: The End of Days.* Carol Stream, Illinois: Tyndale House Publishers, 2004.

LaHaye, Tim and Jerry B. Jenkins. *The Rising: Antichrist Is Born/Before They Were Left Behind.* Carol Stream, Illinois: Tyndale House Publishers, 2005a.

LaHaye, Tim and Jerry B. Jenkins. *The Regime: Evil Advances/Before They Were Left Behind.* Carol Stream, Illinois: Tyndale House Publishers, 2005b.

LaHaye, Tim and Jerry B. Jenkins. *The Rapture: In the Twinkling of an Eye/ Countdown to the Earth's Last Days.* Carol Stream, Illinois: Tyndale House Publishers, 2006.

LaHaye, Tim and Jerry B. Jenkins. *Kingdom Come: The Final Victory.* Carol Stream, Illinois: Tyndale House Publishers, 2007.

LeClaire, Jennifer. *The Spiritual Warrior's Guide to Defeating Water Spirits: Overcoming Demons That Twist, Suffocate, and Attack God's Purposes for Your Life.* Shippensburg, Pennsylvania: Destiny Image Publishers, 2018.

Lindsey, Hal. *The Late Great Planet Earth.* Grand Rapids, Michigan: Zondervan, 1970.

Maiden, John G. *Age of the Spirit: Charismatic Renewal, the Anglo-World, and Global Christianity, 1945–1980.* Oxford, Oxford University Press, 2023.

Marshall, Ruth. *Political Spiritualities. The Pentecostal Revolution in Nigeria.* Chicago: University of Chicago Press, 2009.

Mattera, Joseph. *The Global Apostolic Movement and the Progress of the Gospel.* Ames, Iowa: BILD International, 2022.

McAlister, Elizabeth. "Possessing the Land for Jesus." *Spirited Things: The Work of "Possession" in Afro-Atlantic Religions.* Edited by Paul C. Johnson. Chicago: University of Chicago, 2014, pp. 177–205.

McAlister, Elizabeth. "The Militarization of Prayer in America: White and Native American Spiritual Warfare." *Journal of Religious and Political Practice*, 2.1, 2016, pp. 114–130.

McClain, Alvin J. *Daniel's Prophecy of the Seventy Weeks.* Whitefish, Montana: Kessinger Publishing (Kessinger Legacy Reprints), 2010.

McVicar, Michael J. *Christian Reconstructionism: R. J. Rushdoony and American Religious Conservatism.* Chapel Hill: University of North Carolina Press, 2015.

Meyer, Birgit. "Pentecostalism and Globalization." *Studying Global Pentecostalism. Theories and Methods.* Edited by Allen Anderson, Michael Bergunder, André Droogers, and Cornelis van der Lann. Los Angeles: University of California Press, 2010, pp. 113–130.

Moore, S. David. *The Shepherding Movement: Controversy and Charismatic Ecclesiology.* New York: T&T Clark (Journal of Pentecostal Theology, Supplement Series 27), 2003.

Murphy, Ed. *The Handbook for Spiritual Warfare* (Revised and Updated). Nashville: Thomas Nelson, 2003.

Nel, Marius. "What Is 'the Sign of the Son of Man in Heaven' (Matt. 24:30)?" *In die Skriflig*, 49.1, Art. #1876, 9 pages, 2015. 10.4102/ids.v49i1.1876

Nelson, Anne. *The Shadow Network. Media, Money, and the Secret Hub of the Radical Right.* New York: Bloomsbury, 2019.

Olukoya, Daniel K. *The Mysteries of Life.* Lagos: Battle Cry Christian Ministries, 2010.

Olukoya, Daniel K. *Disgracing Water Spirits: Deliverance Manual for Indigenes of Riverine Areas*. Lagos: Mountain of Fire and Miracles Ministries, 2012.

Onishi, Bradley. *Preparing for War: The Extremist History of White Christian Nationalism – and What Comes Next*. Minneapolis, Minnesota: Broadleaf Books, 2023.

Otis, Jr., George. *The Last of the Giants: Lifting the Veil on Islam and the End Times*. Tarrytown, New York: Chosen Books, 1991.

Otis, Jr., George. *Informed Intercession*. Ventura, California: Renew Books, 1999.

Parham, Charles. *A Voice Crying in the Wilderness*. Baxter Springs, Kansas: Charles Parham, 1902.

Pate, Marvin C., Kenneth L. Gentry, Jr., Sam Hamstra, and Robert L. Thomas. *Four Views on the Book of Revelation*. Grand Rapids, Michigan: Zondervan, 1998.

Paulk, Earl. *Held in the Heavens Until ...* Atlanta, Georgia: K Dimension Publishers, 1985.

Paulk, Earl. *Thrust in the Sickle and Reap*. Atlanta, Georgia: K Dimension Publishers, 1986.

Pierce, Chuck D. and Robert Heidler. *The Apostolic Church Arising: God's People Gathering and Contending for the Glory Today*. Denton, Texas: Glory of Zion International Ministries, Inc., 2015.

Pink, Sarah, Heather Horst, John Postill, Larissa Hjorth, Tania Lewis, and Jo Tacchi. *Digital Ethnography. Principle and Practices*. London: Sage, 2016.

Pivec, Holly and R. Douglas Geivett. *Counterfeit Kingdom: The Dangers of New Revelation, New Prophets, and New Age Practices in the Church*. Nashville: B&H Books, 2022.

Posner, Sarah. *Unholy: Why Evangelicals Worship at the Alter of Donald Trump*. New York: Random House, 2020.

Riss, Richard M. *Latter Rain: The Latter Rain Movement of 1948 and the Mid-Twentieth Century Evangelical Awakening*. Mississauga, Ontario: Honeycomb Visual Productions, 1987.

Robinson, James. "The Healing Ministry in Irvingism." *Divine Healing: The Formative Years, 1830-1890. Theological Roots in the Transatlantic World*. Eugene, Oregon: Pickwick Publications, 2011, pp. 11–39.

Rosenthal, Marvin. *The Pre-Wrath Rapture of the Church*. Nashville: Thomas Nelson, 1990.

Rushdoony, Rousas J. *The Institutes of Biblical Law*. Nutley, New Jersey: The Craig Press, 1973.

Sharlet, Jeff. *The Undertow: Scenes from a Slow Civil War*. New York: W. W. Norton & Company, 2023.

Silvoso, Ed. *Ekklesia: Rediscovering God's Instrument for Global Transformation*. Grand Rapids, Michigan: Chosen Books, 2017.

Stavo-Debauge, Joan. "Mauvaise foi. Du *revival* de la philosophie analytique de la religion à l'introduction de l'objection intégraliste en théorie politique." *Quel âge post-séculier? Religions, démocraties, sciences*. Edited by Joan Stavo-Debauge, Philippe Gonzalez and Roberto Frega. Paris: Éditions de l'EHESS (Raisons pratiques), 2015, pp. 151–182.

Stein, James K. *Philipp Jakob Spener, Pietist Patriarch*. Chicago: Covenant Press, 1986.

Stewart, Adam. "From Monogenesis to Polygenesis in Pentecostal Origins: A Survey of the Evidence from the Azusa Street, Hebden and Mukti Missions." *PentecoStudies*, 32.2, 2014, pp. 151–172.

Stewart, Katherine. *The Power Worshippers: Inside the Dangerous Rise of Religious Nationalism*. New York: Bloomsbury, 2019.

Stoeffler, Ernest. *The Rise of Evangelical Pietism*. Leiden: Brill, 1971.

Strachan, C. Gordon. *The Pentecostal Theology of Edward Irving*. London: Darton, Longman & Todd, 1973.

Tisby, Jemar. *The Color of Compromise: The Truth about the American Church's Complicity in Racism*. Grand Rapids, Michigan: Zondervan, 2019.

Turner, John G. *Bill Bright and Campus Crusade for Christ: The Renewal of Evangelicalism in Postwar America*. Chapel Hill: The University of North Carolina Press, 2008.

Wacker, Grant. *Heaven Below: Early Pentecostals and American Culture*. Cambridge: Harvard University Press, 2001.

Wagner, C. Peter. *Signs and Wonders Today: The Story of Fuller Theological Seminary's Remarkable Course on Spiritual Power*. Altamonte Springs, Florida: Creation House, 1987.

Wagner, C. Peter. *The Third Wave of the Holy Spirit: Encountering the Power of Signs and Wonders*. Ann Arbor: Vine Books, 1988.

Wagner, C. Peter. *Warfare Prayer: How to Seek God's Power and Protection in the Battle to Build His Kingdom*. Ventura, California: Regal Books (The Prayer Warrior Series), 1992.

Wagner, C. Peter. *Confronting the Powers: How the New Testament Church Experienced the Power of Strategic-Level Spiritual Warfare*. Ventura, California: Regal Books, 1996.

Wagner, C. Peter. *The New Apostolic Churches*. Ventura, California: Regal Books, 1998.

Wagner, C. Peter. *Churchquake! How the New Apostolic Reformation Is Shaking Up the Church as We Know It*. Ventura, California: Regal Books, 1999.

Wagner, C. Peter. *Apostles and Prophets: The Foundation of the Church*. Ventura, California: Regal Books, 2000a.

Wagner, C. Peter. *The Queen's Domain: Advancing God's Kingdom in the 40/70 Window*. Colorado Springs: Wagner Publications, 2000b.

Wagner, C. Peter. *Confronting the Queen of Heaven*. Colorado Springs: Wagner Publications, 2001.

Wagner, C. Peter. *Changing Church: How God Is Leading His Church into the Future*. Ventura, California: Regal Books, 2004.

Wagner, C. Peter. *Apostles Today: Biblical Government for Biblical Power*. Bloomington, Minnesota: Chosen Books, 2006a.

Wagner, C. Peter. *The Church in the Workplace: How God's People Can Transform Society*. Ventura, California: Regal Books, 2006b.

Wagner, C. Peter. *Dominion! How Kingdom Action Can Change the World*. Grand Rapids, Michigan: Chosen Books, 2008.

Wagner, C. Peter. *Wrestling with Alligators, Prophets and Theologians: Lessons from a Lifetime in the Church. A Memoir*. Ventura, California: Regal Books, 2010.

Wagner, C. Peter. *Supernatural Forces in Spiritual Warfare: Wrestling Dark Angels*. Shippensburg, Pennsylvania: Destiny Image Publishers, 2012.

Wagner, C. Peter. "Foreword." *Aligning with the Apostolic. Vol. 1*. Edited by Bruce Cook. Houston, Texas: Kingdom House Publishing, 2013a.

Wagner, C. Peter. "Foreword." *Apostolic Centers: Shifting the Church, Transforming the World*. Alain Caron. Colorado Springs: Arsenal Press, 2013b.

Wallnau, Lance. "The Seven Mountain Mandate." *The Reformer's Pledge*. Edited by Ché Ahn. Shippensburg, Pennsylvania: Destiny Image Publishers, 2010, pp. 177–194.

Weaver, John. *The New Apostolic Reformation: History of a Modern Charismatic Movement*. Jefferson, North Carolina: McFarland & Company, Inc., Publishers, 2016.

Weborg, C. John. "Pietism: Theology in Service of Living Toward God." *The Variety of American Evangelicalism*. Edited by Donald W. Dayton and Robert K. Johnston. Eugene, Oregon: Wipf & Stock, 1997, pp. 161–183.

Wesley, John. *A Plain Account of Christian Perfection*. Peabody, Massachusetts: Hendrickson, 2007.

White, Timothy B. "Understanding Principalities and Powers." *Territorial Spirits: Practical Strategies for How to Crush the Enemy through Spiritual Warfare*. Edited by C. Peter Wagner. Shippensburg, Pennsylvania: Destiny Image Publishers, 2012, pp. 83–91.

Whitehead, Andrew L. and Samuel L. Perry. *Taking America Back for God: Christian Nationalism in the United States*. Oxford: Oxford University Press, 2020.

Williams, Daniel K. *God's Own Party: The Making of the Christian Right*. New York: Oxford University Press, 2010.

Wimber, John. *Power Evangelism: Signs and Wonders Today*. London: Hodder and Stoughton, 1985.

NAME INDEX

SUBJECT INDEX

SCRIPTURE INDEX

Printed in the USA
CPSIA information can be obtained
at www.ICGtesting.com
LVHW020805090124
768438LV00004B/289